PRAYERS
FOR
Emotional
Wholeness

365 PRAYERS *for*
LIVING *in* FREEDOM

STORMIE
OMARTIAN

HARVEST HOUSE PUBLISHERS
EUGENE, OREGON

Cover by Koechel Peterson & Associates, Inc., Minneapolis, Minnesota

Author photo © Michael Gomez Photography

PRAYERS FOR EMOTIONAL WHOLENESS
Copyright © 2007 by Stormie Omartian
Published by Harvest House Publishers
Eugene, Oregon 97402
www.harvesthousepublishers.com

ISBN 978-0-7369-2828-1 (pbk.)
ISBN 978-0-7369-3697-2 (eBook)

The Library of Congress has cataloged the edition as follows:

Library of Congress Cataloging-in-Publication Data

Omartian, Stormie.
  Prayers for emotional wholeness / Stormie Omartian.
    p. cm.
  ISBN 978-0-7369-1977-7 (hardcover)
  1. Prayers. I. Title.
  BV245.O43 2007
  242'.8–dc22

                                                        2006025788

Printed in the United States of America

14 15 16 17 18 / BP-NI / 10 9 8 7 6 5 4

Contents

Introduction

$\mathscr{G}$od's purpose for our lives is to make us whole—which is the way He created us to be—and then to work through us for His glory as we surrender our lives to Him. Emotional wholeness means living without negative emotions and having peace about who you are and where your life is headed.

When I was trying to find emotional wholeness for myself, prayer was a big part of that process. That's because when we pray to God, we are spending time in His presence. And in His presence is where we find healing from the pain of our past. It's where we learn to think clearly and maintain a right attitude. It's where we learn to speak words that bring life and not death into our situations and relationships. In His presence is where we learn to make good choices and decisions so we can become productive and fruitful.

Whenever we pray to God, we find His comfort, guidance, peace, love, joy, contentment, forgiveness, hope, and deliverance. We get rid of negative emotions, such as anger, anxiety, depression, doubt, loneliness, fear, and guilt. By praying, we can find help in times of trouble, temptation, weakness, and enemy attack. Prayer is important not only for our own wholeness, but for the healing and wholeness of our relationships as well. Prayer draws us closer to God, where we can get a vision for our future and better understand our purpose.

Who doesn't need all that? I know I do. Even though I have come out of a past of brokenness and feel like a whole person, I still need to pray every day. I know I continue to be a work in progress. Perhaps you feel like a work in progress too. That means you know God has more for you and you want to get rid of anything in your life that keeps you from experiencing it. If so, you will find the prayers and Scriptures in this book to be very helpful. They can be used in your daily prayer walk with God and, I hope, be a starting point from which you share your heart and your specific concerns with Him. My prayer is that they will help you pray in greater detail about the important issues of your life. You can pray these prayers in order—one a day for 365 days—or you can go to specific areas of prayer focus that you know you need to pray about right away.

Every one of us needs more of the wholeness God has for us, because He has far more than we can imagine.

Stormie Omartian

When I Need to Be Free of Anxiety and Depression

*L*ord, I thank You for Your Word because it is good and it gives me life. It puts joy in my heart every time I read it. I pray that Your Word in me will fill my heart with Your love and peace and cause all anxiety, depression, and other dark clouds to blow away from me like ashes in the wind. I ask that You would take away any sadness in my heart and set me completely free from all negative emotions.

Anxiety in the heart of man causes depression, but a good word makes it glad.

PROVERBS 12:25

When I Need to Be Free of Anxiety and Depression

*L*ord, help me to not feel anxious about my future or getting my needs met. Help me to trust that You have brought me this far and that You will bring me the rest of the way. Help me to not worry about things, but to take my concerns to You in prayer instead and leave them in Your hands.

I say to you, do not worry about your life, what you will eat or what you will drink; nor about your body, what you will put on. Is not life more than food and the body more than clothing?

MATTHEW 6:25

When I Need to Be Free of Anxiety and Depression

Dear Lord, because I am Your child, I can refuse to allow depression to settle on me like a heavy blanket. Because I am Yours, I don't have to be weighed down with anxiety. Because Your Spirit lives in me, I have the power to rise above the things that trouble me. Because I love You and Your ways, my life can be renewed every day. Today I pray that You would take away all anxiety, sadness, and depression and renew my mind and emotions.

Unless Your law had been my delight, I would then have perished in my affliction. I will never forget Your precepts, for by them You have given me life.

PSALM 119:92-93

4

When I Need to Be Free of Anxiety and Depression

Lord, I pray that You would take away any sadness I feel and evaporate all depression or oppression that hangs heavily over me. I want to experience Your joy in my soul at all times. I want to feel the lightness of heart I know You have for me. Thank You for bearing my sorrow so I don't have to carry it myself. Help me to experience Your peace that passes all understanding.

Surely He has borne our griefs and carried our sorrows; yet we esteemed Him stricken, smitten by God, and afflicted.

ISAIAH 53:4

When I Need to Be Free of Anxiety and Depression

*L*ord, in the night when I feel anxious about things and I'm tired and overwhelmed with all that I face, it's then that I long for Your presence more than ever. My soul seeks your Holy Spirit—my Comforter—to comfort me. Help me to stay in Your presence both day and night so that I can sense Your freedom from worry at all times.

With my soul I have desired You in the night, yes, by my spirit within me I will seek You early; for when Your judgments are in the earth, the inhabitants of the world will learn righteousness.

ISAIAH 26:9

6

When I Need to Be Free of Anxiety and Depression

Lord, I confess that sometimes I get anxious about whether my needs will be met. Whether I will always have a home to live in and food to eat. Whether I will be able to provide for the family members You have given me to care for. Lord, take away all anxiety and help me to have peace. Help me to no longer worry about the future because I have released it into Your hands.

Do not seek what you should eat or what you should drink, nor have an anxious mind.

LUKE 12:29

When I Need to Be Free of Anxiety and Depression

*L*ord, I put my hope in You. I refuse to look to other things or other people to give me purpose, fulfillment, and peace. I confess any anxiety I have as a lack of trust in Your ability to sustain me. I submit my life to You and put all my expectations in Your goodness, power, and love. Help me to pray about everything and trust You in every part of my life.

My soul, wait silently for God alone, for my expectation is from Him.

Psalm 62:5

When I Need to Be Free of Anxiety and Depression

*L*ord, thank You that whenever my heart is heavy, I can call on You and You will hear me. I know that if You hear my voice, You will answer my prayers. Therefore, I will not allow the enemy of my soul to bring me down and torture me with thoughts that make me anxious, sad, or depressed. I will come to You instead.

I am weary with my groaning; all night I make my bed swim; I drench my couch with my tears. My eye wastes away because of grief; it grows old because of all my enemies. Depart from me, all you workers of iniquity; for the LORD has heard the voice of my weeping.

PSALM 6:6-8

When I Need to Be Free of Anxiety and Depression

Lord, I know that sometimes I worry about things, and You have said I don't need to be anxious about anything but rather to pray about everything. I lift up to You my situation and the things that trouble me most. Take away the burden of them from me and help me see them from Your perspective. Thank You for Your Word that says You will perfect the things that concern me. I put all my trust and confidence in You.

The Lord will perfect that which concerns me.

PSALM 138:8

When I Need to Be Free of Anxiety and Depression

*L*ord, I thank You for Your mercy and that Your mercies are new every morning when I wake up. Thank You that You are faithful to love me unconditionally. Help me to remember that because of Your mercy and love, I have all I need and I can refuse to feel anxiety about the present or future. I just need to pray about them.

Through the LORD's mercies we are not consumed, because His compassions fail not. They are new every morning; great is Your faithfulness.

LAMENTATIONS 3:22-23

When I Need to Be Free of Anxiety and Depression

Lord, take all heaviness of heart away from me. Revive my soul and help me to have a vision for the future. Take anything out of my mind and my life that is not of You. Enable me to be faithful to You and Your ways and to live a life based on the truth of Your Word. Help me to never lie to myself or to others and compromise the life You have for me.

My soul melts from heaviness; strengthen me according to Your word. Remove from me the way of lying, and grant me Your law graciously.

PSALM 119:28-29

When I Need to Be Free of Anxiety and Depression

*L*ord, I thank You that You hear my prayers, my praise, and my thanksgiving to You. Thank You that I can make the desires of my heart known to You and You will hear and answer. I lift up to You everything that concerns me today and ask that You would make it all work out for my greatest good. I am grateful that because of You I don't have to be anxious about anything.

Be anxious for nothing, but in everything by prayer and supplication, with thanksgiving, let your requests be made known to God.

PHILIPPIANS 4:6

When I Need to Be Free of Anxiety and Depression

*L*ord, I confess that there are things that make me feel anxious in my soul. I lift them up to You and ask that You would take those anxieties away and give me Your peace. Comfort my soul as only You can do. Help me to understand my life and my circumstances from Your perspective so that I won't be tempted to dwell on them with a heavy heart. Thank You for the comfort of Your unfailing love.

In the multitude of my anxieties within me, Your comforts delight my soul.

PSALM 94:19

When I Need to Be Free of Anxiety and Depression

Lord, I confess to You that sometimes I feel down, sad, or depressed. But I know You have joy, gladness, peace, and fulfillment for me right where I am. Help me to put my hope in You and praise You in the midst of whatever I experience. Help me to look to You for everything, for You are my God who puts a smile on my face and joy in my heart.

Why are you cast down, O my soul? And why are you disquieted within me? Hope in God; for I shall yet praise Him, the help of my countenance and my God.

PSALM 42:11

When I Need to Be Free of Anxiety and Depression

*L*ord, show me where I have anxious thoughts within me. Search my heart and expose anything that keeps me from the wholeness You have for me. I want to become all You made me to be, and I know that's not possible as long as anxiety rules my heart. Thank You that You did not make me to live with anxiety or sadness, but You created me to find joy in You every day.

Search me, O God, and know my heart; try me, and know my anxieties.

Psalm 139:23

When I Need to Be Liberated from Loneliness

Thank You, Lord, that You are always with me. Help me to remember that at all times, especially when I feel lonely. Because You died for me, Jesus, I know the depth of Your love for me. Because Your Spirit is within me, I always have the comfort of Your presence. Enable me to sense Your presence and love in a greater way than ever before so that I can be lifted out of any loneliness I feel. Take the pain of loneliness away from me forever.

I am with you always, even to the end of the age.

Matthew 28:20

When I Need to Be Liberated from Loneliness

*T*hank You, Lord, that You will never reject me or cast me away from Your presence. Thank You that You always remember me. I am never forgotten by You. You knew me before I was born. Before I ever knew of You, You thought of me. Help me to think of You always too. May my thoughts of Your love set me free from the pain of loneliness. Help me to think of loneliness as a reminder that I need to draw closer to You.

God has not cast away His people whom He foreknew.

ROMANS 11:2

When I Need to Be Liberated from Loneliness

Lord, help me to be content with where I am, knowing that You will not leave me there forever. Help me to never have jealousy or envy because of the love or companionship that someone else has or enjoys. Help me to keep my eyes on You and not on what others do or don't do for me. Thank You that You will never leave me or forsake me.

Let your conduct be without covetousness; be content with such things as you have. For He Himself has said, "I will never leave you nor forsake you."

HEBREWS 13:5

When I Need to Be Liberated from Loneliness

*L*ord, You are the one who knows me best and cares for me most. You are the one who has committed unconditional love to me for eternity. Help me not to fault other people for what I perceive as their not loving me or caring for me as I want them to. Help me to continue to show love to others no matter what their response is to me.

For your Maker is your husband, the LORD of hosts is His name; and your Redeemer is the Holy One of Israel; He is called the God of the whole earth.

ISAIAH 54:5

When I Need to Be Liberated from Loneliness

*T*hank You, Lord, that You are near to me when I call upon You with my whole heart. I call to You today because I need to feel Your love, peace, joy, and power in my life. Thank You, Lord, that Your Holy Spirit lives in me and is with me always, so I don't have to be alone. Help me to sense Your presence now and make me more and more aware of Your healing love each day.

The Lord is near to all who call upon Him, to all who call upon Him in truth.

PSALM 145:18

When I Need to Be Liberated from Loneliness

I come before You now, Lord, asking that You will be close to me and fill me afresh with Your Holy Spirit. Flow through me with Your living water and cleanse my soul of all loneliness. I refuse to be double-minded by thanking You for Your presence and then acting as if You are not there. Take away any pain of feeling alone and help me to sense Your presence in a deeper way. Thank You that You are always loving me to wholeness.

Draw near to God and He will draw near to you. Cleanse your hands, you sinners; and purify your hearts, you double-minded.

JAMES 4:8

When I Need to Be Liberated from Loneliness

*L*ord Jesus, how often You withdrew from other people to be alone. But You were never really alone because You were always with Your heavenly Father. The one time You must have felt deeply alone was when You cried out to God saying, "Why have You forsaken Me?" But You were forsaken so that I will never have to be. Thank You, Lord, for liberating me from loneliness forever.

When Jesus perceived that they were about to come and take Him by force to make Him king, He departed again to the mountain by Himself alone.

JOHN 6:15

When I Need to Be Liberated from Loneliness

*L*ord Jesus, when You were on earth You knew You were never alone because Your heavenly Father was always with You. Help me to have that same ongoing sense of Your presence too. Help me to be so aware of Your presence throughout each day that I can feel Your love taking away any sense of loneliness and healing me to complete wholeness. I know that when I walk with You, I can never truly be alone.

Yet if I do judge, My judgment is true; for I am not alone, but I am with the Father who sent Me.

JOHN 8:16

When I Need to Be Liberated from Loneliness

*L*ord, whenever You went through times of trouble, You always withdrew from the crowd and went to a place by Yourself to be alone with Your heavenly Father. Help me to learn to do that too. At the first sign of loneliness or lack of peace, remind me to draw closer to You and sense the comfort of Your presence and the healing power of Your love.

You have made him most blessed forever; You have made him exceedingly glad with Your presence.

PSALM 21:6

When I Need to Be
Liberated from Loneliness

*L*ord, whenever I am afflicted with loneliness, I know the enemy plays with my mind and makes me think I am unloved or rejected. Thank You that You always love me and never reject me. Thank You that because of Your presence in my life, I don't have to live with loneliness in my heart. Give me the "continual feast" of a heart that is happy no matter the circumstances.

All the days of the afflicted are evil, but he who is of a merry heart has a continual feast.

PROVERBS 15:15

When I Need to Be Liberated from Loneliness

*L*ord, I invite Your presence to invade my life in a fresh, new way. Help me to sense Your presence in greater power and depth than I have ever been able to before. Overflow me with Your love, peace, and joy, and crowd out anything in me that is not Your will for my life. Take away all feelings of separation, rejection, or lack of connection to others, and give me a greater sense of being connected to You.

Teaching them to observe all things that I have commanded you; and lo, I am with you always, even to the end of the age. Amen.

MATTHEW 28:20

When I Need to Be
Liberated from Loneliness

*L*ord, I feel as Moses did. I don't want to go any-
where if Your presence doesn't go with me. I don't want
to spend a moment without Your presence in my life. In
Your presence is peace, joy, rest, fulfillment, and love. In
Your presence I am free from all loneliness and sadness.
Help me to never do anything that would compromise
the fullness of Your presence in my life.

*He said, "My Presence will go with you, and I
will give you rest." Then he said to Him, "If Your
Presence does not go with us, do not bring us up
from here."*

EXODUS 33:14-15

When I Need to Be Delivered from Fear

Lord, I am sometimes afraid of what might happen in the future. I submit all my fears to You and thank You that You will take them from me. I lift up to You my greatest fear and ask that You would give me Your peace in place of that fear. When troubling things happen to me or around me, help me to remember that You are on my side and will fight for me. If You are for me, then no one can ever succeed against me.

You must not fear them, for the LORD *your God Himself fights for you.*

DEUTERONOMY 3:22

When I Need to Be Delivered from Fear

$\mathcal{L}$ord, I thank You that no matter what has happened to me in the past, no matter what is happening in my circumstances now, You promise to never leave me or forsake me. Thank You that because You love me, I don't ever have to live in fear. I pray that You would take away anything in my life that gives me good reason to be afraid. Keep me safe and protected where I am, and take me to a place of safety in the future.

Be strong and of good courage, do not fear nor be afraid of them; for the LORD your God, He is the One who goes with you. He will not leave you nor forsake you.

DEUTERONOMY 31:6

When I Need to Be Delivered from Fear

Thank You, Lord, for Your love in my life. Thank You that Your love takes away all fear. I submit to You the things I fear right now and ask You to take away all torment concerning them. Remove anything that is troubling to me and give me peace. Thank You that Your perfect love, which casts out all fear, is perfecting me even now as I pray. Thank You that Your perfect love is making me whole.

There is no fear in love; but perfect love casts out fear, because fear involves torment. But he who fears has not been made perfect in love.

1 JOHN 4:18

When I Need to Be Delivered from Fear

$\mathscr{L}$ord, the only fear I want to have in my life is the fear of what my life would be like without You. I only want to reverence You, and if I am not doing that fully, then show me how. If I am not living Your way, reveal that to me and I will repent and change my thoughts and actions. Help me to always hold fast to You so that my foundation is secure. I want to be set free of all that keeps me from moving into the life of wholeness You have for me.

You shall walk after the LORD your God and fear Him, and keep His commandments and obey His voice; you shall serve Him and hold fast to Him.

DEUTERONOMY 13:4

When I Need to Be Delivered from Fear

*L*ord, help me not to fear what others think of me. Help me to remember that because You have saved me and Your Spirit lives within me, the things judgmental people say cannot ultimately hurt me. When people say things that are critical, help me to let those things roll off my back and not stay in my mind and heart. Thank You that although hurtful words may come and go, my salvation lasts forever.

Listen to me, you who know righteousness, you people in whose heart is My law: do not fear the reproach of men, nor be afraid of their insults. For the moth will eat them up like a garment, and the worm will eat them like wool; but My righteousness will be forever, and My salvation from generation to generation.

ISAIAH 51:7-8

When I Need to Be Delivered from Fear

*L*ord, I trust in You and refuse to be afraid of anything. You are my salvation and my strength. You are the song that rises in my heart. You have saved me from the hand of the enemy and have given me the power to resist his attacks against my life. Deliver me from the enemy today and every day in the future. I put my life in Your hands and determine to rest in the peace You have for me.

Behold, God is my salvation, I will trust and not be afraid; for YAH, the LORD, is my strength and song; He also has become my salvation.

ISAIAH 12:2

When I Need to Be Delivered from Fear

*L*ord, help me to stand without fear in the midst of the frightening things I face today. Help me to rest in confidence that I will see Your power save me and work for my good. Help me to possess the land You have given me in my life so that the enemy cannot steal from me. Help me to not be dismayed, no matter what happens, because I know You are in charge of my life.

Moses said to the people, "Do not be afraid. Stand still, and see the salvation of the LORD, which He will accomplish for you today. For the Egyptians whom you see today, you shall see again no more forever."

EXODUS 14:13

When I Need to Be Delivered from Fear

When I fear failure, I look to You, Lord, to keep me from falling. Even when I haven't done everything right, I know Your mercy, love, and kindness are extended to me whenever I turn to You. When I feel as though I am falling, I reach to You to pull me up and set me on solid ground. Help me to not fail, but to be successful in all I do. Bless my work and my relationships so that they will prosper and bear much fruit and glorify You always.

If I say, "My foot slips," Your mercy, O Lord, will hold me up.

Psalm 94:18

When I Need to Be Delivered from Fear

*L*ord, set me free from worry about the future and the bad things I fear could happen. Help me to focus instead on the situations I face today and Your great power to see me through each one victoriously. Bless my health, my work, my relationships, my decisions, my finances, my friends, and my family. I place my life fully in Your hands and trust that You, Lord, will help me and guide me on the path to complete wholeness and success in life.

Do not worry about tomorrow, for tomorrow will worry about its own things. Sufficient for the day is its own trouble.

Matthew 6:34

When I Need to Be Delivered from Fear

*L*ord, I lay my fears before You and ask You to set me free from them. Help me to not be led or motivated by fear, but rather to sense Your presence in my life setting me free from all fear. Thank You that You are my God who gives me strength, and that You hold me up and help me to stand in courage in the face of fearful things. Thank You, Lord, that You are far greater than anything I fear.

Fear not, for I am with you; be not dismayed, for I am your God. I will strengthen you, yes, I will help you, I will uphold you with My righteous right hand.

ISAIAH 41:10

When I Need to Be Delivered from Fear

*D*ear Lord, I thank You that You have not given me a spirit of fear. You gave me love and power and a sound mind instead. I reject fear and refuse to be bound up with it, because Your perfect love in me gives fear no place in my life. I refuse to be afraid because You have sent Your power to move on my behalf. And You have given me a clear mind so that I can discern the difference. Help me to remember Your perfect love whenever I am afraid.

God has not given us a spirit of fear, but of power and of love and of a sound mind.

2 TIMOTHY 1:7

When I Need to Be
Delivered from Fear

*L*ord, when I see the things that are happening around me, I become afraid of that happening to me too. When I see tornadoes, hurricanes, and earthquakes, I fear being caught in one. But You, Jesus, rebuked the storm and the sea was calm. And You rebuked Your disciples for being fearful instead of faithful. Lord, help me to have big faith, so that when the storms of life come I will pray in power instead of trembling in fear.

He said to them, "Why are you fearful, O you of little faith?" Then He arose and rebuked the winds and the sea, and there was a great calm.

MATTHEW 8:26

When I Need to Be Delivered from Fear

*L*ord, I see in Your Word that there is the connection between fear and faith. My fears reveal to me that I need to have greater faith in Your ability to protect me and meet my needs. Lord, grow my faith so strong that I am no longer controlled or motivated by fear in any way. Let faith arise in me and dissolve any fear I have. I lift all my fears to You and lay them at Your feet. Help me to release them entirely into Your hands.

He said to them, "Why are you so fearful? How is it that you have no faith?"

MARK 4:40

When I Need to Be Delivered from Fear

*L*ord, You are the light of my life. Because of You I don't need to be afraid of what the forces of darkness try to do to me. You have not saved me for destruction, but for a purpose. Therefore, when fear causes me to feel weak, I will remember that You are the strength of my life. Help me to acknowledge Your power and love at all times so that fear never overtakes me. I pray that You, Lord, will keep me safe from harm or danger at all times.

The Lord is my light and my salvation; whom shall I fear? The Lord is the strength of my life; of whom shall I be afraid?

PSALM 27:1

When I Need to Be Rescued out of Trouble

*L*ord, I thank You that You are my source when I am needy. You are my help in times of trouble. I don't have to be afraid of what troubles may come upon me because You are my hiding place and my source of protection. You are my strength when I feel weak in the face of opposition. Help me to rest in the safety of Your protection and look to You for everything I need in good as well as difficult times.

God is our refuge and strength, a very present help in trouble.

PSALM 46:1

43

When I Need to Be
Rescued out of Trouble

*L*ord, when something happens that is disturbing
to me, I look to You to turn it around for good. Even
though what happens may be a big disappointment to
me, it is also a great opportunity to invite You to turn it
into something positive. I look to You now and ask that
You would bring good out of the things that trouble
me today. May I never be brought to shame by trouble
in my life.

*In You, O LORD, I put my trust; let me never be
ashamed; deliver me in Your righteousness.*

PSALM 31:1

When I Need to Be Rescued out of Trouble

*L*ord, help me to guard my soul from any perverse influence, whether it be from people I associate or work with, or from any media I allow into my home and my life. Give me discernment so that I will not accept as normal something You have declared to be perverse. I don't want to set up a snare for my own soul and invite trouble for my life just because I am around distasteful things in the world and have become desensitized to them. Help me to be sensitive to Your Spirit and what grieves You. Help me to not accept things into my soul that are unacceptable to You.

*Thorns and snares are in the way of the perverse;
he who guards his soul will be far from them.*

PROVERBS 22:5

When I Need to Be
Rescued out of Trouble

*L*ord, I thank You that You will keep me safe and far from trouble. I ask for Your hand of protection to be upon me, especially upon my health, my home, my workplace, and any form of transportation, whether I be in a car, bus, plane, or train, or whether I am walking out on a busy street. Take away all sense of impending doom, whether I am in my home or somewhere else. Help me to sleep in peace at night, knowing You are guarding my dwelling place.

I will both lie down in peace, and sleep; for You alone, O Lord, make me dwell in safety.

PSALM 4:8

When I Need to Be
Rescued out of Trouble

Thank You, Lord, that even if I have to be in a dangerous place, I don't have to fear because You are with me. Help me to never do anything foolish to put You to the test on that. Help me to not put myself in harm's way by my own carelessness, arrogance, or ignorance. But if I must be in a place that seems threatening, I pray You would give me a sense of Your presence and Your protection in it.

The fear of man brings a snare, but whoever trusts in the LORD shall be safe.

PROVERBS 29:25

When I Need to Be Rescued out of Trouble

*T*hank You, Lord, that because You have saved me and I am right with You, my enemy cannot have any victory in my life. You, Lord, are my rock, my strength, and my protector, so there is no one who can destroy my life as long as I walk with You. Thank You that You always hear my prayers and will be my help in times of trouble. I ask You to keep me safe from trouble, harm, or evil influences today and every day.

*He is near who justifies Me; who will contend with Me? Let us stand together. Who is My adversary? Let him come near Me. Surely the Lord G*OD *will help Me; who is he who will condemn Me?*

ISAIAH 50:8-9

When I Need to Be Rescued out of Trouble

*L*ord, in the dark times of my life I turn to You. I know that You are always there to light up my path. Help me to remember that because I trust in You, I don't ever have to walk through troubling situations alone. Take away all dread of my problems and give me a greater sense of Your presence walking me through them. Help me to hear Your voice instructing me, and give me the strength and determination to obey Your directions.

Who among you fears the LORD? Who obeys the voice of His Servant? Who walks in darkness and has no light? Let him trust in the name of the LORD and rely upon his God.

ISAIAH 50:10

When I Need to Be Rescued out of Trouble

Thank You, Lord, that I don't have to run away from trouble and hide in fear. I can instead come to You and ask You to go before me and fight for me against all opposition. I ask You to do that today. Save me from the things I fear will harm me. Thank You that You are my rear guard and You have always got my back. Help me to trust in You and not in my own strength when I am in trouble.

You shall not go out with haste, nor go by flight; for the LORD will go before you, and the God of Israel will be your rear guard.

ISAIAH 52:12

When I Need to Be Rescued out of Trouble

*T*hank You, Lord, that You are always on my side. Thank You that You always choose me for Your team. With You I am eternally loved and accepted. Help me to not be afraid of the trouble that others can bring into my life. I ask You to be my protector. Protect me from the slander of people's words. Protect my reputation. Keep me safe from the plans of evil people. Don't allow the sins of others to destroy my life or the lives of the people I love.

The LORD is on my side; I will not fear. What can man do to me?

PSALM 118:6

When I Need to Be Rescued out of Trouble

*L*ord, I call on Your name this day, for I know my help is in You. God, You are the maker of heaven and earth and all things in-between. You are my Creator, and Your love for me protects me from harm. Jesus, You are my Savior and have saved me for all eternity. Save me out of all troubling situations. Lift me out of any trouble in my life right now. Keep trouble far from me. Holy Spirit, You are my guide. Guide me away from all that is harmful to my life.

Our help is in the name of the LORD, who made heaven and earth.

PSALM 124:8

When I Need to Be
Rescued out of Trouble

*L*ord, I come humbly before You as Your servant and thank You for keeping me safe from trouble. I pray for Your protection upon my health, my mind, my family, my finances, my emotions, and my reputation. Thank You that no weapon formed against me will prosper. Thank You that You have made me to be righteous in Your eyes, and You will protect me from the slander and condemnation of others.

"No weapon formed against you shall prosper, and every tongue which rises against you in judgment you shall condemn. This is the heritage of the servants of the LORD, and their righteousness is from Me," says the LORD.

ISAIAH 54:17

When I Need to Be
Rescued out of Trouble

*L*ord, thank You for being with me in times of trouble. I know that when I cry out to You, You will deliver me. I ask You to deliver me today from all trouble, and to deliver me in the future from the plans of the enemy for my destruction. Give me a long and successful life free from the influences of evil people. Thank You for saving me and loving me enough to hear my prayers and answer them.

He shall call upon Me, and I will answer him; I will be with him in trouble; I will deliver him and honor him. With long life I will satisfy him, and show him My salvation.

PSALM 91:15-16

When I Need to Be
Rescued out of Trouble

Thank You, Lord, for who You are in my life. I reverence You above all else in this world. I know that in my worship and praise and awe of You, there is a flow of Your Spirit that is released to me that brings Your life to flow into mine. This flow of Your life carries me away from the pitfalls of destruction and death. Praising You lifts me above the trouble in my life and into Your presence, where I am safe. Help me to remember to praise You first, no matter what is happening around me.

The fear of the LORD is a fountain of life, to turn one away from the snares of death.

PROVERBS 14:27

When I Need to Be Rescued out of Trouble

*D*ear Lord, help me to be so filled with Your Word, love, power, and peace that even when I am under attack by the enemy, my heart and my faith will not waver. My confidence is in You, Lord, and it cannot be shaken, even by an onslaught of the enemy. Help me to remember that when trouble does come into my life, I don't have to be afraid because You are with me. And You have promised to never leave or forsake me.

Though an army may encamp against me, my heart shall not fear; though war should rise against me, in this I will be confident...For in the time of trouble He shall hide me in His pavilion; in the secure place of His tabernacle He shall hide me; He shall set me high upon a rock.

PSALM 27:3,5

When I Need to Be
Rescued out of Trouble

*L*ord, I lift my hands to You and ask that You would extend Your hands to me and lift me above all the trouble in my life. Take away all fear and torment and help me to openly share my heart with You about all the things that concern me most right now. Thank You that You are always my help in times of trouble, and with You I have nothing to fear. Help me to face each challenge with hope in my heart and not dread.

For I, the LORD *your God, will hold your right hand, saying to you, "Fear not, I will help you."*

ISAIAH 41:13

When I Need to Resist Temptation and Live God's Way

*D*ear God, help me to resist all temptation to disobey You. I don't want to do anything that would keep my prayers from being heard. Help me to not even think about sinning or acting in a way that would displease You. My desire is to do only the things that bring You glory. Enable me to do that. I want to live the way You want me to live so that I can move into all You have for me.

If I regard iniquity in my heart, the LORD will not hear. But certainly God has heard me; He has attended to the voice of my prayer.

PSALM 66:18-19

When I Need to Resist Temptation and Live God's Way

*L*ord, help me to obey You at all times. Put a holy barometer in me that always measures the spiritual climate I am in so that I never compromise Your ways. Warn me whenever I am close to crossing over the line from doing things Your way into doing what is wrong in Your sight. Thank You for the wonderful rewards of peace, wholeness, and fulfillment You give to all those who live according to Your commandments.

The fear of the LORD *is clean, enduring forever; the judgments of the* LORD *are true and righteous altogether…Moreover by them Your servant is warned, and in keeping them there is great reward.*

PSALM 19:9,11

When I Need to Resist Temptation and Live God's Way

*L*ord, I know that life lived by the power of Your Spirit has greater rewards and profits than anything I can accomplish in my own flesh. Help me to always live according to Your Word and to refuse to be tempted to do otherwise. I know that living Your way benefits every part of my life. Help me to live in a godly manner so that I can receive the promises You have for me in this life as well as in the life to come.

Bodily exercise profits a little, but godliness is profitable for all things, having promise of the life that now is and of that which is to come.

1 Timothy 4:8

When I Need to Resist Temptation and Live God's Way

Lord, I can't live without a manifestation of Your presence and Your love to me every day. Each time I feel Your presence and sense Your love, I know I am becoming whole. Help me to express the depth of my love to You by always obeying Your commandments. Help me to follow Your instructions perfectly at all times. Help me to worship You with my whole heart in a way that pleases You.

He who has My commandments and keeps them, it is he who loves Me. And he who loves Me will be loved by My Father, and I will love him and manifest Myself to him.

JOHN 14:21

61

When I Need to Resist
Temptation and Live God's Way

*L*ord, I don't want to ever miss the mark You have for my life by not living Your way. Speak to my heart about any of the plans I have for my life that are causing me to completely miss the plans You have for me. I don't want to assume that I'm doing everything right. I don't want to live my life without asking You how.

He who keeps His commandments abides in Him, and He in him. And by this we know that He abides in us, by the Spirit whom He has given us.

1 JOHN 3:24

When I Need to Resist Temptation and Live God's Way

*L*ord, I pray that I will never do anything foolish that would get me off the path You have for me. Help me to resist temptation to do something that is not right in Your eyes. If I have blamed You for things that have happened, I confess that as sin and ask You to forgive me. Give me the ability to make good choices in everything I do. Take away all foolishness in my heart and give me Your wisdom to guide me in every decision.

The foolishness of a man twists his way, and his heart frets against the LORD.

PROVERBS 19:3

When I Need to Resist Temptation and Live God's Way

*D*ear God, I need Your help in order to be a person of complete truth. I am Your child in whom Your Spirit of truth resides, and I want to live like it. Enable me to resist temptation to be untruthful in any way so that I can keep destruction far from me. I don't want to receive the consequences for telling a lie of any kind. Make me to be a person of truth and integrity that people can trust. Help me to never compromise Your truth in my life.

A false witness will not go unpunished, and he who speaks lies shall perish.

PROVERBS 19:9

When I Need to Resist Temptation and Live God's Way

*L*ord, help me to always seek counsel from people who have godly wisdom so that my decisions and actions will keep me in the covering of Your protection and safety. Help me to be around people who will encourage me to stay on the path You have for me. Help me to recognize and avoid those who will cause me to stray from Your ways. Give me the strength to resist the temptation to go along with the crowd if the crowd isn't going along with You.

Where there is no counsel, the people fall; but in the multitude of counselors there is safety.

PROVERBS 11:14

65

When I Need to Resist Temptation and Live God's Way

Lord, I ask that You would forgive all the ways I have disobeyed Your laws. I don't want to shut off the blessings You have for me by allowing unconfessed sin to have a place in my life. I want to bring everything before You so I can be free of the bondage and death that are the consequences of sin. Show me anything I need to confess and repent of today. Help me turn away from all temptation to disobey You, and enable me to live in the center of Your will every day.

Blessed is he whose transgression is forgiven, whose sin is covered.

PSALM 32:1

When I Need to Resist Temptation and Live God's Way

*L*ord, I come to You to confess the sins that are in my heart and the temptations that cross my mind. Forgive me for any thought that does not glorify You. Take away all desire from my mind and soul to do anything that would grieve Your Spirit. Thank You that Your forgiveness is unending toward those who have a repentant heart and love You more than they love the desires of their flesh. I love You more than all else, and I don't want any sin in my heart and mind to keep me from the wholeness You have for me.

I acknowledged my sin to You, and my iniquity I have not hidden. I said, "I will confess my transgressions to the LORD," and You forgave the iniquity of my sin.

PSALM 32:5

When I Need to Resist Temptation and Live God's Way

*L*ord, help me to give to You all that You want me to. Teach me how to give to others as well. Help me to give of myself, my time, or what I have whenever You instruct me to do so. Show me who You want me to give to and what I should give. I know that giving is a step of obedience, and there is great blessing in giving Your way. Help me to not stop up my life from the free flow of Your Spirit by not giving when and how I should.

Give, and it will be given to you: good measure, pressed down, shaken together, and running over will be put into your bosom. For with the same measure that you use, it will be measured back to you.

LUKE 6:38

When I Need to Resist Temptation and Live God's Way

*D*ear Lord, thank You that You have put Your Spirit in me and You are teaching me to obey Your directions. Help me to keep Your commandments in my heart so that I don't forget to do what's right. I want to live Your way and stay on the path You have for me to walk so that I can receive all that You have for me and prosper in all that I do. Enable me to do Your will every day.

I will put My Spirit within you and cause you to walk in My statutes, and you will keep My judgments and do them.

EZEKIEL 36:27

When I Need to Resist Temptation and Live God's Way

*L*ord, help me to always seek godly counsel. When I need to seek a Christian counselor, show me whom that should be. I love Your laws and Your ways, and I want to live according to Your instructions. Help me to do that. Enable me to make time to be in Your Word every day so that Your laws become part of the fabric of my heart and soul. I want to receive the blessings You give to those who walk according to Your will.

Blessed is the man who walks not in the counsel of the ungodly, nor stands in the path of sinners, nor sits in the seat of the scornful; but his delight is in the law of the LORD, and in His law he meditates day and night.

PSALM 1:1-2

When I Need to Resist Temptation and Live God's Way

*L*ord, help me to know Your Word well enough to speak it out loud whenever I need to recall it. I know that Your Word is living and powerful, and it always accomplishes the purpose for which You have sent it. May Your Word living in me help me to become the whole and productive person You made me to be. May it work in me and prepare me to accomplish great things for Your kingdom.

So shall My word be that goes forth from My mouth; it shall not return to Me void, but it shall accomplish what I please, and it shall prosper in the thing for which I sent it.

ISAIAH 55:11

When I Need to Resist Temptation and Live God's Way

*L*ord, I know Your ways are higher than mine, so I need You to help me make Your ways my ways. Enable me to make Your thoughts my thoughts. Help me to see things in my life from Your perspective so that I can understand the bigger picture and not get mired down in the petty details of life that can get me off the path You have for me.

"For My thoughts are not your thoughts, nor are your ways My ways," says the Lord. "For as the heavens are higher than the earth, so are My ways higher than your ways, and My thoughts than your thoughts."

Isaiah 55:8-9

When I Need to Resist Temptation and Live God's Way

Lord, I believe the Bible is Your Word to me, and I choose to believe it and do what it says. Enable me to see the truth in Your Word and act upon it. Reveal to me all that I need to understand so that I can be changed by it. Write Your Word on my heart so that my heart can be cleansed by it. Help me to deeply understand Your Word so that I can always live Your way.

If anyone wants to do His will, he shall know concerning the doctrine, whether it is from God or whether I speak on My own authority.

JOHN 7:17

When I Need to Resist Temptation and Live God's Way

Dear Lord, I thank You that Your mercy and love are always there for me, even though I don't do things perfectly. Thank You for Your faithfulness and that You are always on my side. Your amazing love for me makes me want all the more to do what pleases You. Help me to obey Your laws and do the things that give You pleasure. I want to walk in the way of mercy and truth. I want Your goodness and mercy to follow me all the days of my life.

All the paths of the LORD are mercy and truth, to such as keep His covenant and His testimonies.

PSALM 25:10

When I Need to Forsake Anger and Gain Patience

*L*ord, give me the ability to be slow to anger. Take away anything in me that refuses to let go of anger over things that have happened. Help me to not get angry over what I think are injustices or personal affronts. Help me instead to quickly overlook the things that make me upset and release all my anger to You. Replace anger in me with Your love and patience. I don't want anger in me to delay my wholeness and keep me from the destiny You have for me.

The discretion of a man makes him slow to anger, and his glory is to overlook a transgression.

PROVERBS 19:11

When I Need to Forsake Anger and Gain Patience

*L*ord, help me to not carry anger in my heart over anything. When someone does something that is offensive to me, enable me to rise above any anger or hurt I may feel over it. Help me to let it go and forgive quickly so that I don't give place to anger in my soul. Enable me to be patient with all people and situations so that I will reflect Your nature and not give place to my flesh.

Cease from anger, and forsake wrath; do not fret;
it only causes harm.

PSALM 37:8

When I Need to Forsake Anger and Gain Patience

Thank You, Lord, that You give me strength to live through each day and face all that I must face. The greatest thing I face today is nothing in light of Your power to give me strength. Strengthen me by the power of Your Spirit to lay down any anger I may have about anything. Give me the ability to be patient with people and situations, and to trust You in the timing of all things. I pray that You will give me patience instead to do all You have called me to do.

I can do all things through Christ who strengthens me.

PHILIPPIANS 4:13

When I Need to Forsake Anger and Gain Patience

I want to be like You, Lord—slow to anger and abounding in mercy. Help me to better understand Your mercy toward me so that I will be able to extend it to others. Help me to be gracious to everyone I see and to be full of compassion in all situations. Keep me from any kind of emotional outbursts or reactions to things that are inspired by my flesh. I want to reflect Your Spirit living in me at all times.

The LORD is merciful and gracious, slow to anger, and abounding in mercy.

PSALM 103:8

When I Need to Forsake Anger and Gain Patience

Lord, help me to always have a kind response to others, even when they are not kind to me. Give me a heart so full of Your love that I am not easily angered by rudeness or insensitivity coming from other people. Help me to not retaliate with angry words that I will ultimately regret and that will grieve Your Holy Spirit. If anyone is angry at me for any reason, whether justified or not, help me to always give a soft and gentle answer and forsake harsh words that stir up strife. Enable me to live in peace with the people around me.

A soft answer turns away wrath, but a harsh word stirs up anger.

PROVERBS 15:1

When I Need to Forsake Anger and Gain Patience

*G*od, help me to not stir up any strife between me and the people around me. I don't want to be in a contentious situation with anyone. Enable me to have such a patient and loving heart that I am never quick to have words with a person or blow up at anyone. Instead, make me slow to anger. Help me to be a peacemaker so I can move into the blessings and wholeness You have for me.

A wrathful man stirs up strife, but he who is slow to anger allays contention.

PROVERBS 15:18

When I Need to Forsake Anger and Gain Patience

*L*ord, I confess that it takes great strength for me to rule over my spirit. I pray that You would give me that kind of strength so I will be able to take control of my emotions. I don't want to be ruled by them in any way. Help me to never have an angry outburst or say things I regret. Help me to not hold anger in and make myself sick with it, either. Give me such a compassionate, loving, and patient heart toward others that I am not even tempted to show anger toward anyone.

He who is slow to anger is better than the mighty, and he who rules his spirit than he who takes a city.

PROVERBS 16:32

When I Need to Forsake Anger and Gain Patience

*L*ord, help me to be like Abraham and patiently endure all that's necessary in order to see Your will accomplished in my life. I don't want to let anger over a situation shut off or delay anything You want to do in me. I don't want to be like people whose own anger keeps them from moving into all You have for them. I don't want to let my own impatience keep me from receiving the promises You have for me.

When God made a promise to Abraham, because He could swear by no one greater, He swore by Himself saying, "Surely blessing I will bless you, and multiplying I will multiply you." And so, after he had patiently endured, he obtained the promise.

HEBREWS 6:13-15

When I Need to Forsake Anger and Gain Patience

*L*ord, I know that having patience makes me more complete. And having anger shatters my life. I choose to have patience in all things so that I can be complete and whole, lacking nothing, just as Your Word promises. Enable me to forsake all anger in my life and not give place to it for even a moment. I don't want to compromise the perfecting process You have begun in me. Help me to react with patience to the situations in my life.

Let patience have its perfect work, that you may be perfect and complete, lacking nothing.

JAMES 1:4

When I Need to Forsake Anger and Gain Patience

Lord, when it seems that I am trying my best to do the right thing and then accused of something I haven't done, or I have had my actions or words misunderstood in some negative way, please help me to not get upset about it. Help me, instead, to have a patient and understanding heart. Help me to assume the best about people and not the worst. Help me to be quick to forgive and show patience.

What credit is it if, when you are beaten for your faults, you take it patiently? But when you do good and suffer, if you take it patiently, this is commendable before God.

1 PETER 2:20

When I Need to Forsake Anger and Gain Patience

Lord, help me to glorify You by overlooking all offenses against me. Give me the patience I need to not react. Give me the discretion I need to be able to calmly choose the way of peace and not anger as a way to respond. Keep me from destroying my life or shutting off all You have for me by showing anger and making bad choices because of it. Fill me with Your love, peace, and joy every day and help me to always choose to live in them.

Let all bitterness, wrath, anger, clamor, and evil speaking be put away from you, with all malice. And be kind to one another, tenderhearted, forgiving one another, even as God in Christ forgave you.

EPHESIANS 4:31-32

When I Need to Forsake Anger and Gain Patience

*L*ord, help me to never give place to jealousy in any way. Help me to be so filled with Your love, peace, and joy that envy over anything never enters my heart or my mind. Help me to be loving and kind at all times so that I never fall prey to the cruelty of my own wrath. Don't allow the torrential power of anger to wash away my life in a moment of weakness. Give me patience and peace in my heart because I look to You for all I need.

Wrath is cruel and anger a torrent, but who is able to stand before jealousy?

PROVERBS 27:4

When I Need to Forsake Anger and Gain Patience

*L*ord, I know that I can't always see the whole picture in any situation, but You can. Help me to be patient to see a situation through to the end instead of being quick to judge without finding out all the facts. Help me to not succumb to prideful anger, but rather to be humble and patient in spirit, always giving others the benefit of the doubt. Help me to never be prideful in my dealings with others, but to always extend to them the mercy and grace You have extended to me.

The end of a thing is better than its beginning; the patient in spirit is better than the proud in spirit.

ECCLESIASTES 7:8

When I Need to Forsake Anger and Gain Patience

*L*ord, help me to be patient with everyone. If I have to say something to someone about potentially upsetting things, help me to do it with love and graciousness. Help me to be compassionate, comforting, and uplifting to people and not impatient or abrasive. Take any anger out of my heart and replace it with Your kindness and love. May the fruit of Your Spirit be manifested in me at all times.

Now we exhort you, brethren, warn those who are unruly, comfort the fainthearted, uphold the weak, be patient with all.

1 THESSALONIANS 5:14

When I Need to Forgive and Get Free of the Past

*L*ord, show me if there is anyone from whom I need to ask forgiveness. If there is anything hurtful I may have said or done to someone, whether knowingly or not, I pray You will bring it to my understanding so I can confess it to You and that person and be forgiven. Bring to mind anything I have promised to someone that I have not followed through on so I can make amends. I want to clear the air in all my relationships. Show me anyone I need to pray with or for, with regard to any unforgiveness between us. I want to know the healing that forgiveness brings.

Confess your trespasses to one another, and pray for one another, that you may be healed. The effective, fervent prayer of a righteous man avails much.

JAMES 5:16

When I Need to Forgive and Get Free of the Past

*L*ord, I want to always be open and clean before You in my heart. I want to confess everything I need to repent of so that I can receive Your full forgiveness. Show me if I am trying to hide anything from You or anyone else. Cleanse my heart of all unrighteousness so that I can live fully in Your presence and receive all the wholeness You have for me. I want to have the beautiful countenance of someone who is completely right before You.

I acknowledged my sin to You, and my iniquity I have not hidden. I said, "I will confess my transgressions to the LORD," and You forgave the iniquity of my sin.

PSALM 32:5

When I Need to Forgive and Get Free of the Past

Lord, where I have been judgmental or condemning of others, I ask You to forgive me. Help me to forgive all offenders against me—past, present, and future. I don't want anything to stand in the way of my receiving Your full forgiveness in my life. If I have in any way blamed You for something that has happened, reveal that to me so I can confess that misplaced blame as well. I don't ever want anything to come between You and me, especially my own unforgiveness.

Judge not, and you shall not be judged. Condemn not, and you shall not be condemned. Forgive, and you will be forgiven.

LUKE 6:37

When I Need to Forgive and Get Free of the Past

*J*esus, give me the ability to love those who have hurt me, to bless those who have been cruel to me, and to be good to those who have behaved badly toward me. Help me to pray for the people I least want to pray for. I am Your child, and I want to inherit Your ability to show love and mercy at all times.

I say to you, love your enemies, bless those who curse you, do good to those who hate you, and pray for those who spitefully use you and persecute you, that you may be sons of your Father in heaven.

MATTHEW 5:44-45

When I Need to Forgive and Get Free of the Past

*L*ord, help me to love others the way You love them. On earth, Jesus, You even loved those who hated, tortured, and killed You. You forgave them without hesitation. Help me to do that too. Help me to forgive even those who have hurt me, hated me, or used me. Help me to let go of resentment or bitterness. Above all, take away any thought I may ever have of revenge or getting even or rejoicing at another's downfall. Help me to truly forgive and love my enemies. Only by the power of Your Spirit will I be able to do that.

Jesus said, "Father, forgive them, for they do not know what they do." And they divided His garments and cast lots.

LUKE 23:34

When I Need to Forgive and Get Free of the Past

*L*ord, help me to be the kind of person who allows people to change or be different than they are at the moment. Help me to pray for people instead of judging them. I want to release people into Your hands and not bring condemnation back on myself by holding them to me with my unforgiveness. Enable me to forgive people as often as it takes, just as You have said to do in Your Word.

If he sins against you seven times in a day, and seven times in a day returns to you, saying, "I repent," you shall forgive him.

LUKE 17:4

When I Need to Forgive and Get Free of the Past

*L*ord, You have forgiven me for so much. You have taken my sin and covered it completely with Your blood. And now my sin is just as if it never happened. Help me to always remember that Your forgiveness has set me free so that I will forgive others just as completely and set them free from *me*. Help me to never try and hold people to myself by not forgiving them. I don't want to experience the emotional sickness that withholding forgiveness brings. I want to know the freedom and wholeness that comes with forgiving others.

Blessed is he whose transgression is forgiven, whose sin is covered.

PSALM 32:1

When I Need to Forgive and Get Free of the Past

*L*ord, I want to be cleansed of anything in my life that is unrighteous or unholy. Specifically, I want to confess to You any unforgiveness I may have. Bring to my mind anyone or anything that I need to release from my life by forgiving them. I want to be free of all that is not Your way for me so that I can step out of the past and into the future You have for me. Thank You that when I confess my sins, You are faithful to forgive me and cleanse my heart of all that is not holy.

If we confess our sins, He is faithful and just to forgive us our sins and to cleanse us from all unrighteousness.

1 JOHN 1:9

When I Need to Forgive and Get Free of the Past

Lord, I know that I can never be whole as long as I have not confessed my sin before You and received Your full forgiveness. Bring to mind anything I am doing or thinking that I need to confess to You now. If I have allowed my mind to wander to places it shouldn't have, show me and I will confess it. If I have said or done things that are offensive or have caused You or others grief, I want to repent of all that so I can be made right before You and whomever I have offended or hurt. Help me to be completely free of all sin in my life so I don't have to suffer the pain and destruction that sin brings.

Look on my affliction and my pain, and forgive all my sins.

PSALM 25:18

When I Need to Forgive and Get Free of the Past

*L*ord, I pray that You will help me to show mercy to others just as You have shown mercy to me. Help me to not be judgmental and condemning of other people, but rather enable me to choose the way of acceptance and forgiveness. I want to forgive others so that I can receive full forgiveness from You and release for my own sins. I pray that You would help other people to forgive me for things I have done toward them, whether unintentionally or not. Give me the ability to make things right with people quickly and completely.

Blessed are those whose lawless deeds are forgiven, and whose sins are covered.

ROMANS 4:7

When I Need to Forgive and Get Free of the Past

*L*ord, I know I can't come before You in prayer if I have held anything against anyone and have not forgiven them. If there is a situation like that in my life, show me now as I pray or reveal to me anyone I need to forgive so that I can do that. I don't want to forfeit Your forgiveness of my sin and stop the flow of Your Spirit in my life by not forgiving others as You have instructed me to do.

Whenever you stand praying, if you have anything against anyone, forgive him, that your Father in heaven may also forgive you your trespasses.

MARK 11:25

When I Need to Forgive and Get Free of the Past

*L*ord, help me to let go of the past. I want to make room for the new things You are doing in my life. Help me to forgive myself for times I have failed. I release all memories of that to You and ask You to heal them. Show me the good You have brought out of those times or will bring out of them in the future. Thank You that You have made a way out of the wilderness of my past. Thank You for watering the dry areas of my life with the flow of Your Spirit.

Do not remember the former things, nor consider the things of old. Behold, I will do a new thing, now it shall spring forth; shall you not know it? I will even make a road in the wilderness and rivers in the desert.

Isaiah 43:18-19

When I Need to Forgive and Get Free of the Past

*D*ear Lord, I pray that You would help me to forget the bad and hurtful memories of the past. Whatever negative memory has tried to torment or control me, I release that into Your hands right now. Help me to go forward to all that You have for me now and in the future. Help me to read my past like a history book, so that I can learn from it. Help me to not live there any longer.

I do not count myself to have apprehended; but one thing I do, forgetting those things which are behind and reaching forward to those things which are ahead.

PHILIPPIANS 3:13

When I Need to Forgive and Get Free of the Past

*L*ord, I know that I will never find the wholeness You have for me if I bind up my life with unforgiveness. Help me to forgive people and release them into Your hands. Reveal to me anything I need to see that is keeping my mind and heart in the past. I don't want to experience the torture in my mind, soul, and body that comes with bitterness and unforgiveness. Help me to let go of all bad memories so that I can be completely free of the past and walk unhindered into my future with You.

His master was angry, and delivered him to the torturers until he should pay all that was due to him. So My heavenly Father also will do to you if each of you, from his heart, does not forgive his brother his trespasses.

MATTHEW 18:34-35

When I Need Hope and Joy in My Heart

*L*ord, help me to not look at the lives of others and feel that my life falls short. Help me to not envy others who don't seem to suffer as I have or struggle in the ways that I do. Help me to refuse to allow self-pity to dominate my emotions. Thank You, Lord, that my hope is in You. It will not ever be cut off because I will be with You forever.

Do not let your heart envy sinners, but be zealous for the fear of the LORD all the day; for surely there is a hereafter, and your hope will not be cut off.

PROVERBS 23:17-18

When I Need Hope and Joy in My Heart

Lord, I thank You for Your Word because it gives me comfort and hope. When I lose hope or become discouraged, I pray that You would help me to better understand Your Word and enable me to draw on all the hope that is to be found in it. Help me to know You better so that I can fully understand how great my hope is in You. The hope I find in Your Word gives me joy in my heart.

Whatever things were written before were written for our learning, that we through the patience and comfort of the Scriptures might have hope.

ROMANS 15:4

When I Need Hope and Joy in My Heart

*T*hank You, Jesus, that You paid the ultimate price for me so that I might be redeemed and have joy forever. Because of the joy You have put in my heart, sorrow and trouble have to flee from me. I ask You, Lord, to take all heaviness from my soul and anoint me with the oil of gladness right now. Take all the worries and concerns that are burdens upon me and replace them with never-ending joy.

The ransomed of the LORD shall return, and come to Zion with singing, with everlasting joy on their heads. They shall obtain joy and gladness; sorrow and sighing shall flee away.

ISAIAH 51:11

When I Need Hope and
Joy in My Heart

I submit this day to You, Lord, and all that is in it. This is the day that You have made, and I will rejoice and be glad in it. I refuse to entertain any negative thoughts. Help me to not give place to fear or depression. I will not dread any part of this day but will find only joy, peace, and purpose in all of it. Thank You, Lord, for all that this day holds because I know it is good.

This is the day the LORD has made; we will rejoice and be glad in it.

PSALM 118:24

When I Need Hope and Joy in My Heart

*L*ord, help me to remember all You have done for me. You have been there to help me when I needed You most. Help me to not doubt that You will continue to be there for me in the future. I draw close to You and hide myself in the shadow of Your wings, which will always be a place of refuge for me. I rejoice and give praise and thanks to You that I have this eternal place of safety in You.

Because You have been my help, therefore in the shadow of Your wings I will rejoice.

PSALM 63:7

When I Need Hope and Joy in My Heart

Lord, I have learned to seek You early. Not only early in the day but also early in every situation that arises. Help me to put my hope in You immediately in all circumstances so that discouragement never takes root. Help me to be in Your Word every day so that I can find the hope that is there within it. Make it come alive in my heart so I can understand it and retain it. When I cry out to You for help, I have confidence that You will answer me. That's why my hope is always in You.

I rise before the dawning of the morning, and cry for help; I hope in Your word.

PSALM 119:147

When I Need Hope and Joy in My Heart

*L*ord, I pray that the fruit of Your Spirit will manifest powerfully in my heart and in my life. Fill me with Your love, peace, and joy. Enable me to be patient, kind, and good. Teach me to be faithful and gentle, and help me to have self-control at all times. Control my life so much, Lord, that all these qualities are revealed in me and seen clearly by others. Bring fruitfulness into my life today in every way possible.

The fruit of the Spirit is love, joy, peace, longsuffering, kindness, goodness, faithfulness, gentleness, self-control. Against such there is no law.

GALATIANS 5:22-23

When I Need Hope and Joy in My Heart

*L*ord, there have been times in my life when I have not gotten what I hoped and prayed for and I was heart-sick over it. I know now, though, that my hope is only in You. What You want me to have, You will bring into my life as I walk closely with You. What does not belong in my life, I know You will take away. Help me to fully trust You no matter what happens. Help me to remember that because my hope is in You, I will never be cut off from the blessings You have for me.

Hope deferred makes the heart sick, but when the desire comes, it is a tree of life.

PROVERBS 13:12

When I Need Hope and Joy in My Heart

Dear Lord, I look to You and nothing else. Help me to stay close to You, because I know that if I do, I will always be standing on solid ground. No matter what happens today, help me to keep my heart and mind focused on You. Regardless of what tries to shake up my life, I know that You are in charge of all that happens to me. Your presence brings me joy and gladness and peace because of the hope I have in You.

I have set the LORD always before me; because He is at my right hand I shall not be moved. Therefore my heart is glad, and my glory rejoices; my flesh also will rest in hope.

PSALM 16:8-9

When I Need Hope and Joy in My Heart

God, I praise You this day and proclaim You to be Lord over my life. Thank You for Your mercy and love to me. Even when I am going through a dark night of the soul and have tears that seem to be without end, I know there will come a new morning and joy once again will rise in my heart. I pray now that You will evaporate any oppression that threatens to overtake me. Fill me afresh with Your joy and hope.

Sing praise to the LORD, you saints of His, and give thanks at the remembrance of His holy name. For His anger is but for a moment, His favor is for life; weeping may endure for a night, but joy comes in the morning.

PSALM 30:4-5

When I Need Hope and Joy in My Heart

*L*ord, I thank You that You have bought me with a price and I have an eternal future with You. Even though I may experience times of sorrow, when I sing praise to You, Your joy and peace fill my heart. Pour out an increased portion of Your joy and gladness in me today so that it will overflow onto others I meet. Help me to sing Your praise, even if it has to be only silently in my heart at that moment. Thank You that my hope is in You and Your joy in me is everlasting.

The ransomed of the LORD shall return, and come to Zion with singing, with everlasting joy on their heads. They shall obtain joy and gladness, and sorrow and sighing shall flee away.

ISAIAH 35:10

When I Need Hope and Joy in My Heart

*D*ear God, sometimes I feel at a loss about what to do in my life. Sometimes I don't know if I can do what I know I need to do or what I feel You have called me to do. But the promise in Your Word to Your people who follow You is that we will go forth with peace and things will open up and work out. I pray just that—that You would give me peace and joy as a sign that I am moving in the right direction. I thank You in advance for making things work out for good in my life.

You shall go out with joy, and be led out with peace; the mountains and the hills shall break forth into singing before you, and all the trees of the field shall clap their hands.

ISAIAH 55:12

When I Need Hope and Joy in My Heart

*D*ear God, help me to always be right in my heart before You. Help me to do the things I need to do in order to live according to Your laws. Shine Your light on my path and lead me in the way You have for me to go. Thank You for the gladness of heart You give me whenever I think of You. I praise Your name and exalt You above all else in the world and in my life.

Light is sown for the righteous, and gladness for the upright in heart. Rejoice in the LORD, you righteous, and give thanks at the remembrance of His holy name.

PSALM 97:11-12

When I Need Hope and Joy in My Heart

Dear Lord, I praise You and worship You above all else. Thank You for inhabiting my praise, for it is only in Your presence that I can experience the fullest measure of joy to be found on this earth. I invite Your presence into my life in a greater way than ever before. I ask You to walk with me and lead me in the way You want me to go. Help me to stay close to You, so that I don't ever stray from the plans You have for me. Being with You brings hope and joy to my heart. Being in the presence of Your holiness brings wholeness to my life.

You are holy, enthroned in the praises of Israel.

PSALM 22:3

When I Need Hope and Joy in My Heart

Lord, there is nothing that gives me greater joy than worshipping You. There is nothing more fulfilling, healing, and enlightening than giving You praise. Worshipping You invites Your presence into my life in greater measure. Thank You that when I am in Your presence, You share Yourself with me. You pour all that You are into my soul and spirit. Whenever I am in Your presence, I can feel Your wholeness making me whole. Help me to remember to praise You at the first sign of hopelessness or loss of joy. Help me to make worship of You my first response to all that happens in my life.

They worshiped Him, and returned to Jerusalem with great joy.

LUKE 24:52

When I Need Hope and Joy in My Heart

*D*ear Lord, I come to You with a humble heart, grateful for all You have done for me. Thank You that You are a God who gives me more than I deserve. I ask that You would lift any sadness or heaviness of heart from me today and cause Your joy to rise in my heart instead. Let Your joy so increase in me that it crowds out all else that is negative. Heal any broken places in my soul and restore what has been lost so that I can move into the wholeness You have for me.

The humble also shall increase their joy in the LORD, and the poor among men shall rejoice in the Holy One of Israel.

ISAIAH 29:19

When I Need Hope and Joy in My Heart

$\mathcal{L}$ord, I lift up to You all my concerns and any areas of my life where I have unrest. I ask that You would take this burden away from me and bring Your joy and peace into my life. My hope is in You, and I praise You for Your hand of blessing on me. Thank You that as I look to You, You shine the light of Your face on me and on the path I need to walk. My hope is in You, and I will look to no other one to guide me.

Why are you cast down, O my soul? And why are you disquieted within me? Hope in God, for I shall yet praise Him for the help of His countenance.

PSALM 42:5

When I Need Hope and Joy in My Heart

*L*ord, help me to be so strong in You that my hope never wavers. Help me to never lose hope, even when it seems You have not heard my prayers or things are not going the way I prayed they would. I trust You to answer my prayers in Your way and in Your time. Give me patience to wait on You in faith, knowing that You will not leave me where I am forever. I trust that when things change, they will change for the better. I have joy because my hope is in You.

I will hope continually, and will praise You yet more and more.

PSALM 71:14

When I Need Hope and Joy in My Heart

Lord, You are my God of hope. I hope in You and I find hope in Your Word. I pray that You would so fill me with Your hope, joy, peace, and faith that I become strong and unwavering. Help me not to be shaken or become weak in any of these areas when difficult things happen. No matter how negative the people around me are, help me to remain strong in the positive attributes of hope, joy, peace, and faith. By the power of Your Spirit, help me to overflow with Your love toward others every day.

May the God of hope fill you with all joy and peace in believing, that you may abound in hope by the power of the Holy Spirit.

ROMANS 15:13

When I Need Hope and Joy in My Heart

Lord, I put my trust in You and thank You that You are my defender and protector. I ask that You would protect me from all evil influences and dangers. Come to my defense against the plans of the enemy to destroy my life. I love You, Lord, and I put my trust in You. It gives me great joy to know that You hear my prayers and will answer them because of my love for You and the reverence I have for Your name.

Let all those rejoice who put their trust in You; let them ever shout for joy, because You defend them; let those also who love Your name be joyful in You.

PSALM 5:11

When I Need Hope and Joy in My Heart

*L*ord, I confess that my hope is always in You. Help me to hold on tight to You and not waver, no matter what is happening in or around me. Regardless of what storms arise, let me not be shaken and drawn toward doubt. I trust in Your Word and the promises You have there for me. Thank You that You are always faithful to keep Your promises. Give me the patience, peace, and confidence to wait for Your perfect timing in all things.

Let us hold fast the confession of our hope without wavering, for He who promised is faithful.

HEBREWS 10:23

When I Need Hope and Joy in My Heart

*L*ord, I love experiencing the pleasure of Your company because I find joy in Your presence. Come fill me afresh with Your Holy Spirit right now so that Your joy rises up in my heart and crowds out all sadness and oppression. I know that joy does not depend on circumstances; it depends on my openness to allowing Your Spirit to have control in my life. Lord, I surrender my life to You today. Make me to be known as a person of great joy.

You will show me the path of life; in Your presence is fullness of joy; at Your right hand are pleasures forevermore.

PSALM 16:11

When I Need Hope and Joy in My Heart

Lord, my hope is in You because I am Your child. Purify my heart and make me more like You each day so that I can become all You made me to be. Let hope rise up in my heart so powerfully that no matter what happens, I will not stumble; rather, I will look to You as the answer to all my needs. May Your hope and joy in my heart bring a peace, contentment, and wholeness that I have never dreamed possible.

Beloved, now we are children of God; and it has not yet been revealed what we shall be, but we know that when He is revealed, we shall be like Him, for we shall see Him as He is. And everyone who has this hope in Him purifies himself, just as He is pure.

1 JOHN 3:2-3

When I Need Hope and Joy in My Heart

*L*ord, I choose to believe Your Word, which says that because I have received You and follow You, I will have peace, love, and joy. When I don't feel peaceful or sense Your hope and joy, help me to not trust my feelings. Help me to trust Your Word instead and not allow a work of the enemy try to steal all that from me. Set me free from any wrong thinking so that I can move into the hope and joy You have for me.

Be of good courage, and He shall strengthen your heart, all you who hope in the LORD.

PSALM 31:24

When I Need to Be Free of Guilt and Condemnation

*L*ord, I want to always obey Your commandments and do what pleases You. Show me when I am not doing that. Help me to resist the temptation to do wrong and enable me to do what's right. Teach me to be repulsed by sin. I don't want to live with a heavy heart of condemnation. I want my heart to always be clean before You. I don't want to ever restrict Your answers to my prayers or limit what I can receive from You by not walking in Your ways. Help me to do what is pleasing in Your sight.

Whatever we ask we receive from Him, because we keep His commandments and do those things that are pleasing in His sight.

1 JOHN 3:22

When I Need to Be Free of Guilt and Condemnation

Lord, I know that guilt and condemnation are weights my shoulders were not meant to carry. This kind of weight breaks down my life instead of building it up. I don't want anything to separate me from You and the healing and wholeness You have for me. Show me any sin in my life so that I can confess it, repent of it, and find the refreshing You have for me.

Repent therefore and be converted, that your sins may be blotted out, so that times of refreshing may come from the presence of the Lord.

ACTS 3:19

When I Need to Be Free of Guilt and Condemnation

*L*ord, I confess all of my sins of thought, word, or action to You. Bring anything I have done that does not bring You pleasure or has grieved Your Spirit to my mind right now so that I can repent of it and be free. I don't want guilt or condemnation to hinder my wholehearted worship of You and my ability to be a beacon of Your light to other people. I want to wash my hands in innocence, as Your Word says, so that I can come before Your throne in worship and thanksgiving.

I will wash my hands in innocence; so I will go about Your altar, O Lord, that I may proclaim with the voice of thanksgiving, and tell of all Your wondrous works.

PSALM 26:6-7

When I Need to Be Free of Guilt and Condemnation

*L*ord, create in me a clean heart and deliver me from all guilt and condemnation in my life. I know that You have made a way for me to be free from condemnation and guilt through confession and repentance. Where I have sin to confess, reveal it to me. I want to always have a pure heart toward You. If I have already confessed and repented of the things I feel guilty about, I recognize that this condemnation comes from the enemy of my soul, who wants to put that crushing burden on me. Thank You, Lord, that You have set me free from that burden and I can live confident in Your love for me.

Beloved, if our heart does not condemn us, we have confidence toward God.

1 JOHN 3:21

When I Need to Be Free of Guilt and Condemnation

*L*ord, give me wisdom about the things I "approve of" or "go along with" in life. If I have compromised Your laws in any way, show me so I can make things right. Reveal all my sins to me so I can confess them before You. Where I have feelings of guilt because of something I blame myself for—something I wish I would have done or *not* done—help me to release those feelings into Your hands so that I can be free from the burden of them. Take away any weight of guilt from my life. I want to live my life completely free of condemnation.

Do you have faith? Have it to yourself before God. Happy is he who does not condemn himself in what he approves.

ROMANS 14:22

When I Need to Be Free of Guilt and Condemnation

*L*ord Jesus, thank You that You did not come to earth to condemn me but rather to save me. Help me to remember Your great salvation and mercy in my life. Help me to focus on the freedom I have in You and refuse to allow the enemy to weigh me down with guilt over the sins and failures from which You have already paid the price to set me free. Thank You for saving and redeeming me and restoring my life to wholeness.

God did not send His Son into the world to condemn the world, but that the world through Him might be saved.

JOHN 3:17

When I Need to Be Free of Guilt and Condemnation

*L*ord, You are my Redeemer. You have redeemed my soul from the pit of hell. Thank You for Your Word that says because I have trusted in You, I will not be condemned. I will never have to live in guilt. So I ask You today to set me free from any guilt I feel about things that have happened in the past. Help me to forgive myself for my own failures. They are burdens too heavy for me to carry. Thank You that You redeem all things.

The LORD redeems the soul of His servants, and none of those who trust in Him shall be condemned.

PSALM 34:22

When I Need to Be Free of Guilt and Condemnation

*D*ear Lord, I thank You that You are a merciful God to me. Forgive me for any time I have not shown that same mercy to others. I don't want to be unforgiving or do anything that is not Your way for me. Bring to my mind any occasion where I have been unmerciful so that I can confess it as sin. I want to be set free from all the condemnation and guilt that failure brings.

Judgment is without mercy to the one who has shown no mercy. Mercy triumphs over judgment.

JAMES 2:13

When I Need to Be Free of Guilt and Condemnation

*L*ord, even though I try to do the right thing, I often fail to do so. Help me to overcome my sinful nature by the power of Your Spirit and the truth of Your Word. Help me to not wallow in self-pity, mourning my own failures and inadequacy. Help me to not say or do something that is totally selfish because I want to satisfy my own desires. Help me to have a clean conscience toward You and others at all times.

This being so, I myself always strive to have a conscience without offense toward God and men.

ACTS 24:16

When I Need to Be Free of Guilt and Condemnation

*D*ear Jesus, I thank You with my whole heart that because I have received You and You have forgiven me of my sins, there is no more condemnation for me. Any guilt or condemnation I feel is either because of the enemy of my soul or unconfessed sin in my life. Help me to quickly confess any sin in my life to You. Enable me to continually walk in the Spirit and not in the flesh every day.

There is therefore now no condemnation to those who are in Christ Jesus, who do not walk according to the flesh, but according to the Spirit.

ROMANS 8:1

When I Need to Be Free of Guilt and Condemnation

*D*ear Lord, I know I am responsible for the things I do, think, and say, but I still need Your help in order to do, think, and say things that are a blessing to others and that glorify You. I pray that You would help me to never be critical of others. I don't want to bring condemnation upon myself—especially when it is only by Your grace that I escape the traps of sin. Help me to instead uplift and encourage people and pray for them when they hurt me.

You are inexcusable, O man, whoever you are who judge, for in whatever you judge another you condemn yourself; for you who judge practice the same things.

ROMANS 2:1

When I Need to Be Free of Guilt and Condemnation

*L*ord, I am so grateful for my life in Christ. Thank You that the law of the Spirit of life has made me free from the law of sin and death. Now I don't have to suffer the consequences of sin, but I can enjoy a full life lived in the Spirit instead of an ever-diminishing life lived in the flesh. Enable me to make the right choices so I can be free of guilt and become more alive every day.

For the law of the Spirit of life in Christ Jesus has made me free from the law of sin and death.

ROMANS 8:2

When I Need Deliverance and Restoration

*L*ord, I ask You to deliver me from anything that should not be a part of my life. I invite You to purify and cleanse my heart and set me free from all that keeps me from the life of fulfillment and purpose You have for me. Restore what has been lost to me as only You can do. When I go through the fire, overflow me with Your Spirit so that I am refreshed. When I feel as though I am struggling to stay above water, lift me above my circumstances and bring me safely through to the other side.

You have caused men to ride over our heads; we went through fire and through water; but You brought us out to rich fulfillment.

PSALM 66:12

When I Need Deliverance and Restoration

*L*ord, help me to share with others all that You have done to bring restoration into my life. Help me to tell of the freedom I now experience and *will* experience in my soul in the future. Redeem all areas that have been broken. Restore everything that has been lost. Renew the things in my life that have been worn down and weakened, and make me a testimony to the wholeness You have for those who follow You. I pray You would continue to do great things in me.

Come and hear, all you who fear God, and I will declare what He has done for my soul.

PSALM 66:16

When I Need Deliverance and Restoration

*T*hank You, Lord, that wherever I am locked up in my life, You have the keys to set me free. Whenever I am oppressed, You will bring justice. And whenever I have need, You will supply it. Without You, I am a prisoner of my needs and the consequences of my sin. I pray that You will deliver me from whatever keeps me from becoming all You made me to be.

Happy is he who has the God of Jacob for his help, whose hope is in the LORD his God, who made heaven and earth…who executes justice for the oppressed, who gives food to the hungry. The LORD gives freedom to the prisoners.

PSALM 146:5-7

When I Need Deliverance and Restoration

Lord, I pray that You would deliver me from everything that separates me from You and keeps me from the life You have for me. Thank You that You have delivered my soul from anything that would lead to my destruction. I pray that You will continue to deliver me from all that would bring me down and destroy me. Deliver me from death, failure, and destruction. Deliver me, also, from the things that would bring me grief and cause my life to be diminished in any way. Put me on solid ground in the center of Your will.

You have delivered my soul from death, my eyes from tears, and my feet from falling.

PSALM 116:8

When I Need Deliverance and Restoration

*T*hank You, Lord, that You are a God of redemption and restoration. Thank You that You are restoring my soul. Without the deliverance and restoration You have worked in my life, I don't want to even imagine where I would be today. Continue to lead me in Your paths of righteousness for Your glory so that I can become more like You. I pray You will continue to work deliverance in me and bring restoration to my life until I am complete—just as You created me to be.

He restores my soul; He leads me in the paths of righteousness for His name's sake.

PSALM 23:3

When I Need Deliverance and Restoration

*D*ear God, I thank You that You have saved me so that I don't have to live this life—or my life in eternity—without You. Thank You that You have redeemed my past and given me an eternal future with You forever. Anything I have done outside of Your will or apart from Your guidance I confess as sin and ask You to forgive me and restore me to wholeness. Thank You for Your everlasting kindness and mercy to me. Separate me from anything that would separate me from You.

"With a little wrath I hid My face from you for a moment; but with everlasting kindness I will have mercy on you," says the Lord, your Redeemer.

ISAIAH 54:8

When I Need Deliverance and Restoration

*L*ord, I love and revererence You, and I thank You that I am Your child. You are my heavenly Father who loves me, and Your love is the foundation of my life. You are the rock upon which I stand. I ask that You would work great deliverance in me and free me from everything I need to let go of today. Reveal to me anything that I have yet to recognize as bondage. You are my deliverer. Open my eyes to see anything in my life that is not of You so that I can be free of it.

Because he has set his love upon Me, therefore I will deliver him; I will set him on high, because he has known My name.

PSALM 91:14

When I Need Deliverance and Restoration

*L*ord, I realize that I can do everything I know in the flesh to battle against the things that bind me, but it is only Your delivering power that can truly set me free. That's why I turn to You today and ask You to deliver me from anything in me and in my life that separates me from You or keeps me from becoming all You created me to be. Restore to me all that has been lost in the days that I didn't live for You. Restore everything that the enemy has stolen from my life.

The horse is prepared for the day of battle, but deliverance is of the LORD.

PROVERBS 21:31

When I Need Deliverance and Restoration

*L*ord, You are the only one in the entire world who restores His people to wholeness. Help me to never do anything to stand in the way of Your doing that in me. I don't want to be the kind of person who disobeys You without repentance or an effort to change. Wherever I have become stuck in one place or have become imprisoned in my soul, deliver me today. I don't want to be prey for the enemy or robbed of all You have for me. Set me free and restore me to the whole person You created me to be.

This is a people robbed and plundered; all of them are snared in holes, and they are hidden in prison houses; they are for prey, and no one delivers; for plunder, and no one says, "Restore!"

ISAIAH 42:22

When I Need Deliverance and Restoration

Thank You, Lord, that You are my Redeemer. You are my Creator, the maker of all things. Thank You that You are a God of restoration and I can be built up and restored to complete wholeness. Thank You that I can be filled to overflowing with Your healing love and goodness. Lord, I pray that You would take the broken pieces of my life and make them into something beautiful. Take all that has been wasted in my life and turn it around to count for something good.

Thus says the LORD, your Redeemer, and He who formed you from the womb...who says to Jerusalem, "You shall be inhabited," to the cities of Judah, "You shall be built, and I will raise up her waste places."

ISAIAH 44:24-26

When I Need Deliverance and Restoration

Jesus, deliver me from all selfishness, fear, doubt, anger, and any desire to sin against You in any way. Show me any place in my life where I have held onto sin and I will confess it, renounce it, repent of it, and turn toward Your ways. I know I can't make room in my heart for Your kingdom if I don't make room in my heart for the way You want me to live. Deliver me from anything that keeps me from all You have for me.

In those days John the Baptist came preaching in the wilderness of Judea, and saying, "Repent, for the kingdom of heaven is at hand!"

MATTHEW 3:1-2

When I Need Deliverance
and Restoration

*L*ord, deliver me from the hands of the enemy. Save me from the plans of evil to destroy my life. I trust in You and ask You to help me be set free from anything and anyone who would try to harm me in any way. I thank You that You are my protector and the liberator of my soul. If ever I am tempted to step out from under the covering of Your protection, deliver me from that temptation too. Thank You for restoring me to complete wholeness.

The LORD shall help them and deliver them; He shall deliver them from the wicked, and save them, because they trust in Him.

PSALM 37:40

When I Need Deliverance and Restoration

*L*ord, You are my Savior and deliverer, and I need You to save me and deliver me right now. Set me free from my fears and replace them with new faith. Deliver me from old thoughts and replace them with Yours. Liberate me from memories that serve no good in my life. Replace them with memories of Your goodness to me. Help me learn to praise and worship You for all that You are to me. Help me to remember to thank You often every day for all that You are doing in my life.

Be pleased, O LORD, to deliver me; O LORD, make haste to help me!

PSALM 40:13

When I Need Deliverance and Restoration

*L*ord, I am poor in spirit without You. But with You I am rich and prosperous in my soul. I ask that You would help me in my time of need. Pour out Your Spirit afresh in my heart and help me to experience Your complete deliverance and restoration in my life. I confess that I get impatient because I want to have total freedom and wholeness now. Give me patience to wait on Your timing for everything.

I am poor and needy; yet the LORD thinks upon me. You are my help and my deliverer; do not delay, O my God.

PSALM 40:17

When I Need Deliverance and Restoration

*L*ord, I thank You for the truth of Your Word. Your truth sets me free from all the lies of the enemy, who has tried to bind up my life with false evidence against me. Help me to know more and more of Your truth. Give me greater knowledge of Your Word so that I can always refute the devil's lies. Help me to clearly understand the Bible every time I read it so that Your Word and Your truth will live in me and I will truly be Your disciple.

Jesus said to those Jews who believed Him, "If you abide in My word, you are My disciples indeed. And you shall know the truth, and the truth shall make you free."

JOHN 8:31-32

When I Need Deliverance and Restoration

*D*ear Jesus, I thank You that You willingly were bound and crucified so that I could be free. And I know that You not only freed me from death and hell for eternity, but You also continue to set me free in different ways every day. Thank You, Lord, that when You set me free, it is a complete work and I don't ever have to again go into bondage to that thing from which I was liberated. Help me to live in the freedom, deliverance, and restoration You have for me. Show me anything I need to be free of today.

If the Son makes you free, you shall be free indeed.

JOHN 8:36

154

When I Need Deliverance and Restoration

*L*ord, I thank You for the liberty You have given me. You have set me free from so much already, and I know You will continue to liberate me from things I am not even aware of now. Deliver me today from any yoke of bondage on my life, and help me to stand strong when the enemy tries to entrap me. Keep me from ever being drawn back into any bondage from which You have liberated me.

Stand fast therefore in the liberty by which Christ has made us free, and do not be entangled again with a yoke of bondage.

GALATIANS 5:1

When I Need Deliverance and Restoration

*L*ord, I hide myself in You and ask that You would keep me far from trouble. Deliver me from the enemy's plan for my destruction. Thank You that You surround me with songs of deliverance. I sing praise to You as a battle cry against any attack of the enemy, for I know that worship and praise are songs of deliverance. I worship You as my Creator, deliverer, protector, and provider. I praise You for Your joy, peace, love, provision, and freedom in my life.

You are my hiding place; You shall preserve me from trouble; You shall surround me with songs of deliverance.

PSALM 32:7

When I Need to Renew My Mind

*L*ord, help me to be transformed by the power of Your Spirit. Renew my mind so that it is only filled with Your truth and thoughts that glorify You. I want to be in Your perfect will with everything I do and all that I think. Help me to not compromise the life You have for me by thinking profanely, as the world thinks. Enable me to have thoughts that keep me on the path You have for my life.

Do not be conformed to this world, but be transformed by the renewing of your mind, that you may prove what is that good and acceptable and perfect will of God.

ROMANS 12:2

When I Need to Renew My Mind

*L*ord, I thank You that You have given me a sound mind. I lay claim to it now, and I refuse anything less. Help me to not let my own thoughts control me or cause me to feel down, powerless, or afraid. Enable me to always reject thoughts of evil or of anything that is not glorifying to You. Renew my mind today and make it to be completely sound, sane, and solid. Give me a mind that is full of Your love and compassion—a mind that thinks of others first before myself.

God has not given us a spirit of fear, but of power and of love and of a sound mind.

2 Timothy 1:7

When I Need to Renew My Mind

*L*ord, I praise You and worship You above all things. You are Lord over my life, and I invite You to be Lord over my thoughts as well. I don't want to have any ungodly, foolish, or futile thoughts in my mind at any time. I don't want my thoughts to control my life unless they are thoughts of You and Your Word. Help me to make praise and worship an ongoing part of my life so that wrong thoughts never find a place to reside in my mind.

Although they knew God, they did not glorify Him as God, nor were thankful, but became futile in their thoughts, and their foolish hearts were darkened.

ROMANS 1:21

When I Need to Renew My Mind

*L*ord, help me to think about things that are good and true, which means I can't dwell on lies and bad news. Help me to think on things that are just and pure, which means I can't dwell on evil and impure things. Help me to think loving thoughts and not thoughts of jealousy, anger, or hatred. Help me to think about positive things that are good and worthy of praise, and not allow negative thoughts to permeate my mind and bring confusion. Help me to control my mind at all times.

Whatever things are true, whatever things are noble, whatever things are just, whatever things are pure, whatever things are lovely, whatever things are of good report, if there is any virtue and if there is anything praiseworthy; meditate on these things.

PHILIPPIANS 4:8

When I Need to Renew My Mind

*L*ord, help me to be in unity with other believers. Bring me into harmony with those who love You. Where I or other people are not thinking correctly, I pray that You would literally change our mind so that we are in alignment with You. Help all of us who are called by Your name to be of one mind toward one another so we can continually be moving in the Spirit and not the flesh.

Now I plead with you, brethren, by the name of our Lord Jesus Christ, that you all speak the same thing, and that there be no divisions among you, but that you be perfectly joined together in the same mind and in the same judgment.

1 Corinthians 1:10

When I Need to Renew My Mind

*L*ord, help me to be renewed in my mind so I can become the new person in Christ You have made me to be. I know this cannot happen without Your enablement. So by the power of Your Spirit moving in me and by the power of Your Word finding residence in my mind and heart, I let go of old ways of thinking. Give me clean thoughts that are productive and fruitful. Give me a good memory and the ability to think things through. Give me, I pray, both intelligence and wisdom. Renew my mind to where it needs to be in order to do all You have called me to do.

Be renewed in the spirit of your mind.

EPHESIANS 4:23

When I Need to Renew My Mind

*L*ord, help me to not misuse my time and my mind thinking thoughts that are a futile waste of time. Help me instead to think high-minded thoughts—thoughts that are creative and productive. I give control of my mind to You, Lord, and ask that You would fill it with Spirit-filled thoughts. Don't let wrong thinking lead me astray and alienate me from the life You have for me. Renew my mind with Christlike thoughts and give me the ability to perceive things clearly.

You should no longer walk as the rest of the Gentiles walk, in the futility of their mind, having their understanding darkened, being alienated from the life of God, because of the ignorance that is in them, because of the blindness of their heart.

EPHESIANS 4:17-18

163

When I Need to
Renew My Mind

*L*ord, may the mind that was in Christ Jesus also be in me. Give me the mind of Christ and help me to think clearly, calmly, and righteously. Fill my mind with understanding, wisdom, love, and peace. Take away all thoughts of fear, dread, evil, sin, retaliation, selfishness, criticism, and lies. Help me to not waste my time on thoughts that have no purpose and do nothing to build up my life. Make me whole in my mind so I can think Christlike thoughts that glorify You.

Let this mind be in you which was also in Christ Jesus.

PHILIPPIANS 2:5

When I Need to Renew My Mind

*L*ord, grow me up to have Your mind and Your perspective in all things. If there is anything in my mind that shouldn't be there, any thoughts I should not be thinking, any mind-sets that are wrong, reveal them to me so that I can change my mind and conform it to Yours. Help me to be mature in my thoughts and not foolish. Help me to have creative thoughts that lead to a life of productivity and wholeness.

Let us, as many as are mature, have this mind; and if in anything you think otherwise, God will reveal even this to you.

PHILIPPIANS 3:15

165

When I Need to
Renew My Mind

Lord, I submit my mind to You and ask You to be Lord over it. Help me to think about You, about serving You, and spending eternity with You. Help me to think about Your ways and Your love and Your purpose for my life. Help me to get my mind off of earthly things that have no meaning and no lasting benefit and think about helping others and doing Your will. Take away all confusion and give me a clear, peaceful, and intelligent mind so that I can accomplish great things for Your kingdom.

Set your mind on things above, not on things on the earth.

COLOSSIANS 3:2

When I Need to Renew My Mind

*L*ord, help me to be clear minded, focused, and sober about my walk with You. Protect my mind from scattered thoughts. Help me keep my mind from wandering to thoughts that are not glorifying to You. Make my mind to conform to Yours so that Your will is accomplished through me. I trust in You, Lord, and thank You that because of Your mercy and grace, I can become the person You want me to be.

Gird up the loins of your mind, be sober, and rest your hope fully upon the grace that is to be brought to you at the revelation of Jesus Christ.

1 PETER 1:13

When I Need to Renew My Mind

*D*ear Jesus, I thank You that by the power of Your Spirit I can rule over my sinful nature. With my mind I can choose to live a life in the Spirit and not in the flesh. Help me to be strong in my mind and not weak, so that my mind will always control my flesh and I will not fall away from the life You have for me. Renew my mind today and flush out any thoughts that shouldn't be there. Help me to fill my mind with the truth of Your Word.

I thank God; through Jesus Christ our Lord! So then, with the mind I myself serve the law of God, but with the flesh the law of sin.

ROMANS 7:25

When I Need to Renew My Mind

*L*ord, I ask that You would put Your laws in my mind and engrave them on my heart so that they will keep me on the path You have for me. I want only to be led by Your Spirit and not by my flesh. I want to not only read Your Word but to understand it with my mind and put it to good use in my life. Help me to be a doer of Your Word and not just a listener only. Engrave Your Word deeper in my heart every time I read it.

This is the covenant that I will make with the house of Israel after those days, says the LORD: I will put My laws in their mind and write them on their hearts; and I will be their God, and they shall be My people.

HEBREWS 8:10

When I Need to Renew My Mind

*D*ear Lord, how grateful I am that You have given me the mind of Christ. That is the only way I can understand Your Word and Your revelation to my life. By the power of Your Spirit living in me, guide me and teach me in all that I need to know so that I can grow in the things of Your kingdom. Help me to have the mind of Christ in every decision I make and all that I do.

"Who has known the mind of the LORD that he may instruct Him?" But we have the mind of Christ.

1 CORINTHIANS 2:16

When I Need Victory over My Enemy

Thank You, Lord, that You have given me authority over all the power of the enemy. Help me to remember this when I feel weak or threatened by his attacks. Help me learn how to use the authority You have given me to defeat him every time he encroaches upon my life. Enable me to trample the things that rise up against me and threaten to destroy me. Thank You that Your Spirit in me is greater than all the plans of the enemy. Thank You, Lord, that You will never let the enemy destroy me.

Behold, I give you the authority to trample on serpents and scorpions, and over all the power of the enemy, and nothing shall by any means hurt you.

LUKE 10:19

When I Need Victory over My Enemy

*L*ord, show me how to resist the enemy in every area of my life. Enable me to resist his lies by having a full knowledge of the truth of Your Word. Enable me to resist his temptations by knowing Your commandments. Enable me to avoid his traps by the knowledge and wisdom You give me. Thank You, Jesus, that You defeated the enemy when You were crucified on the cross and You have given me authority over him. Because of You I now have the power to resist him, and when I do, he must flee from me.

Submit to God. Resist the devil and he will flee from you.

JAMES 4:7

When I Need Victory over My Enemy

*L*ord, help me to stand firm on the everlasting foundation I have in You. No matter what whirlwind of attack the enemy sends out against me, I pray it will pass and I will have victory over him. What might wash other people away who don't know You will not shake me. That's because You have put me on a solid foundation in the center of Your will, far from enemy control. Thank You that no matter what happens, my foundation is in You and it will last forever. After all that happens to me or around me, I will be left standing.

When the whirlwind passes by, the wicked is no more, but the righteous has an everlasting foundation.

PROVERBS 10:25

When I Need Victory over My Enemy

Lord, I praise You and thank You that You are more powerful than any enemy I will ever face. I call upon You today and ask You to save me from my enemy. When the enemy comes against me, I will lift up praise to You as a barrier against him. You are far greater than his threats, and I thank You that You will always show Your power on my behalf when I call on You. I worship You amid all that I face today.

I will call upon the LORD, *who is worthy to be praised; so shall I be saved from my enemies.*

PSALM 18:3

When I Need Victory over My Enemy

*L*ord, I thank You that because I am Your servant, no weapon the enemy tries to use against me can prosper. Even when people who are used by the enemy try to do or say things in judgment against me, You will condemn them. Thank You that Your righteousness, Jesus, is a covering for me because You died in my place. Your righteousness in my life protects me from the things that would seek to destroy me.

"No weapon formed against you shall prosper, and every tongue which rises against you in judgment You shall condemn. This is the heritage of the servants of the LORD, and their righteousness is from Me," says the LORD.

ISAIAH 54:17

When I Need Victory over My Enemy

*L*ord, help me to strongly resist the plans of the enemy. Keep me from ever playing into his hand and unwittingly helping him achieve his goals. Help me to be vigilant in prayer so that he will have no opening to devour my life. Help me remember to pray for others who face this same opposition, for I know we have a common enemy. Thank You, Lord, that we also all have the same heavenly Father.

Be sober, be vigilant; because your adversary the devil walks about like a roaring lion, seeking whom he may devour. Resist him, steadfast in the faith, knowing that the same sufferings are experienced by your brotherhood in the world.

1 Peter 5:8-9

When I Need Victory over My Enemy

*L*ord, I pray that You will always be on my side in every battle with the enemy of my soul. If You are with me, I will always have victory. If You are with me, I don't need to be afraid or grow weak in the face of an attack. You give me strength to stand, and You will always show Yourself more powerful than any opposition I have. Help me in the battle I face today. Thank You in advance for the victory You will accomplish on my behalf.

He shall say to them, "Hear, O Israel: today you are on the verge of battle with your enemies. Do not let your heart faint, do not be afraid, and do not tremble or be terrified because of them."

DEUTERONOMY 20:3

When I Need Victory over My Enemy

Dear Lord, I pray that You will always keep me protected from the snare of the devil so that I am never taken captive by him to do his will. I know You will do that because I am Your child and You love me. Help me to never do anything careless or stupid that would cause me to come out from under the covering of Your protection that You give to those who love You and live Your way.

A servant of the LORD must not quarrel but be gentle to all, able to teach, patient, in humility correcting those who are in opposition, if God perhaps will grant them repentance, so that they may know the truth, and that they may come to their senses and escape the snare of the devil, having been taken captive by him to do his will.

2 TIMOTHY 2:24-26

When I Need Victory over My Enemy

Thank You, Lord, that You are my deliverer. I ask that You would deliver me from all attacks of the enemy, both now and in the future. Save me from his traps and evil plans. I put my life in Your hands and trust that You will protect me from all harm or danger. You are my Savior, Redeemer, protector, and provider, and all I need I find in You. When I sense the enemy encroaching upon my life, I pray that You would help me rise up against him in faith, refusing to let him ever discourage or overpower me.

O my God, I trust in You; Let me not be ashamed; let not my enemies triumph over me.

PSALM 25:2

When I Need Victory Over My Enemy

*T*hank You, Lord, for Your hand of protection in my life. I pray that You would keep me out of the way of evil and far from violence and crime. Lift me above any situation that would threaten my safety or the safety of those I care about. Deliver me from any enemy attack or plans for my destruction. Thank You, Lord, that You are almighty and all-powerful, and nothing is too hard for You.

He delivers me from my enemies. You also lift me up above those who rise against me; You have delivered me from the violent man.

PSALM 18:48

When I Need Victory over My Enemy

*L*ord, I praise and worship You as Almighty God, Creator of all things. I worship You as my heavenly Father who is greater than any other. I thank You for being my Savior and protector who lifts me above the reach of my enemy. When I am under enemy attack, I ask that You would remind me to praise You immediately and not give place to fear or doubt. Make me so strong in faith that the enemy does not cause me concern, because my greatest concern is serving You.

My head shall be lifted up above my enemies all around me; therefore I will offer sacrifices of joy in His tabernacle; I will sing, yes, I will sing praises to the LORD.

PSALM 27:6

When I Need Victory over My Enemy

*L*ord, You are my deliverer and I trust Your timing on my deliverance from the hand of the enemy in my life. Liberate me from all persecution and harassment. Set me free from every evil work. Preserve me for the work You have for me to do. Where I have invited the enemy in by compromise or disobedience to Your ways, show me so I can change and make things right. Thank You that You will never deliver me to the will of my enemy.

My times are in Your hand; deliver me from the hand of my enemies, and from those who persecute me.

PSALM 31:15

When I Need Victory over My Enemy

*L*ord, thank You that You will deliver me out of all my trouble and save me from my enemy because I am Yours and I love You and want to live Your way. You have said in Your Word that for all who look to You, You will open Your hand and satisfy the desires of their heart. I ask that You would satisfy the desire of my heart that the enemy be defeated completely in my life. Help me to rise up powerfully against him so that he has no penetration into my life in any way.

For He has delivered me out of all trouble; and my eye has seen its desire upon my enemies.

PSALM 54:7

When I Need Victory over My Enemy

*L*ord, You have delivered me many times from the hand of the enemy. I wouldn't even be alive today without You. The enemy's plan for my destruction would have succeeded if it had not been for You defeating him. I am so grateful that You have redeemed me out of the enemy's hand forever. Help me to tell others of Your deliverance and redemption in my life. Help me to comfort those who hide in fear because of enemy torment. Help me to tell them that what You have done for me, You can do for all who look to You.

Let the redeemed of the LORD say so, whom He has redeemed from the hand of the enemy.

PSALM 107:2

When I Need Victory over My Enemy

Lord, I thank You for all the times You have hidden me from the enemy. You are a strong tower that I can run to whenever I sense the encroachment of evil into my life. I don't have to live in fear because I can come to You in prayer and praise, and You will shelter me from any enemy onslaught. Today I ask You to keep me safe and protected from all evil so that I can be free to grow in service to You and become all You made me to be.

You have been a shelter for me, a strong tower from the enemy.

PSALM 61:3

When I Need Victory over My Enemy

*L*ord, I come to You today and thank You that the victory in my life has already been won over the enemy. Thank You, Jesus, that You loved me enough to die for me so I could be saved. Thank You, God, that You are always on my side. That knowledge gives me great comfort and healing in my soul. Because of You I don't have to be afraid of the enemy's plans against me. Reveal to me anything I need to see about the plans of evil for my life. Show me when and how to pray in order to stay completely protected under Your covering.

When I cry out to You, then my enemies will turn back; this I know, because God is for me.

PSALM 56:9

When I Need Help in Tough Times

*T*hank You, Lord, that You protect me every day of my life, far more than I even know. Thank You that You are more powerful than any enemy I face. Thank You that You go before me whenever I go through difficult situations. Thank You that You are always with me and You will not leave me or forsake me, so I don't need to be afraid of tough times. Give me courage and faith to meet even the most difficult situations I face today.

The LORD, He is the one who goes before you. He will be with you, He will not leave you nor forsake you; do not fear nor be dismayed.

DEUTERONOMY 31:8

When I Need Help in Tough Times

*T*hank You, Lord, that there is power in Your name. I call upon Your name today and ask that You would protect me from all plans of the enemy and any person or circumstance that would be a setup for my downfall. Jesus, I run to You as my strong tower, my refuge in times of trouble. Keep me safe, I pray. I speak the name of Jesus over my situation now. I proclaim that You, Jesus, are Lord over my life and Lord over everything that happens to me.

The name of the Lord is a strong tower; the righteous run to it and are safe.

PROVERBS 18:10

When I Need Help
in Tough Times

*L*ord, help me to rise above the things that concern me. I surrender the burden of them to You and thank You that as I do, You will make the burden light and get me through each difficult situation successfully. I lift my eyes from the problems I face and focus on You and Your love instead. Thank You that although human love fails, Your love never will. Help me to rest in Your love as I watch You bring good out of the tough times in my life.

Cast your burden on the LORD, and He shall sustain you; He shall never permit the righteous to be moved.

PSALM 55:22 NIV

When I Need Help in Tough Times

*L*ord, I worship You above all things. I praise You and proclaim that You are Lord over everything in my life. Thank You that You are more powerful than any of life's storms that I must walk through. I ask You to help me in the situation I am in now and the difficult things I face. I pray that You will give me the desires of my heart concerning these situations. Thank You, Lord, that when I cry out to You, You hear my prayers and will answer.

She came and worshiped Him, saying, "Lord, help me!"

MATTHEW 15:25

When I Need Help in Tough Times

*L*ord, I come before Your throne right now with confidence, knowing that because I am Your child, Your mercy is extended to me. I need Your mercy and grace to be manifested in my life in great measure today. I face difficult things, and I know I cannot meet these challenges without Your help. Enable me to walk through them successfully or lift me out of them completely. I know You will bring good out of the difficult times I go through, and I thank You for the miracles You will do in my life in the process.

Let us therefore come boldly to the throne of grace, that we may obtain mercy and find grace to help in time of need.

HEBREWS 4:16

When I Need Help in Tough Times

*D*ear Lord, I look to You to be all the help I will ever need. Even though I see no other help on the horizon, I will not be afraid or concerned. Even though I may not see a way out, or a good solution to certain problems, I know that *You* do. So I will keep my eyes on You. For You are the Creator of heaven and earth and all that is in them, so I know You are well able to create solutions to my problems. I praise You and thank You that nothing is too hard for You.

I will lift up my eyes to the hills; from whence comes my help? My help comes from the LORD, who made heaven and earth.

PSALM 121:1-2

192

When I Need Help in Tough Times

Lord, my hope is in You. No matter how I feel or what is happening, I always have cause for celebration because You are in charge of my life. I refuse to give in to negative thoughts about my situation, because I know that You will always bring good out of the difficult things I go through. Your Word says that the suffering I feel will seem like nothing in light of the great work You will do in me as a result. So I pray that You will help me face all the challenges of my life with strength and courage and reveal Your glory in me through it all.

For I consider that the sufferings of this present time are not worthy to be compared with the glory which shall be revealed in us.

ROMANS 8:18

When I Need Help in Tough Times

Lord, I pour out my heart before You just as Your Word says to do. I trust in You; You are my refuge. Thank You, Lord, that You hear my prayers and will always answer. I release the burden of all the difficult things that are on my heart into Your hands, knowing that You are the only One who can lift it off and carry it for me. Help me refuse to again pick up and carry any burden I have surrendered to You.

Trust in Him at all times, you people; pour out your heart before Him; God is a refuge for us.

PSALM 62:8

When I Need Help in Tough Times

*L*ord, when things happen that are troublesome and disturbing to me, help me to see the bright side of all of it. Help me to look above my circumstances to Your goodness, mercy, and love. Help me to focus on the power of Your mighty hand and the way You can touch, change, and transform my problems. Turn whatever seems frightening or negative to me into something positive and great. Make these situations work for good in my life and turn them into a blessing as only You can do.

Judge nothing before the time, until the Lord comes, who will both bring to light the hidden things of darkness and reveal the counsels of the hearts. Then each one's praise will come from God.

1 Corinthians 4:5

When I Need Help in Tough Times

*L*ord, whenever grief over something that has happened tries to come back and torture me, I ask that You would take it away and give me peace. Thank You that You are a compassionate God, and You not only see my trouble and grief and understand my loss, but You extend Your hand to me and hear my prayers. I ask that You would unlock all the pain that is captured in my memory and set me free from it. Help me to see that life goes on because You go on and Your compassions never fail.

You, O God, do see trouble and grief; you consider it to take it in hand. The victim commits himself to you; you are the helper of the fatherless.

PSALM 10:14 NIV

When I Need Help
in Tough Times

*L*ord, I thank You that You have set me free from the prison of my own soul. You have brought me out of darkness into Your wonderful light. Thank You that You comfort me by satisfying the hunger and thirst of my soul in dry times. When the heat is on, You protect me. And You not only mercifully lead me, but You also take me to a place of refreshing. I need to experience that place of refreshing today. I pray that You would either take me out of the difficult situations I face or help me go through them to great victory.

They shall neither hunger nor thirst, neither heat nor sun shall strike them; for He who has mercy on them will lead them, even by the springs of water He will guide them.

ISAIAH 49:10

When I Need Help in Tough Times

*D*ear Lord, I am determined to do as Your Word says and count it all joy when I go through trials. I praise You in the midst of the difficult problems I face at this time and proclaim You to be Lord over each one and Lord over my life. I ask that You would be in charge of these situations and bring good out of them. If You are testing my faith, then let patience be revealed in me as I wait for a good end or a satisfying conclusion to each problem. Help my trust in You to not waver through it all.

My brethren, count it all joy when you fall into various trials, knowing that the testing of your faith produces patience.

JAMES 1:2-3

When I Need Help in Tough Times

*L*ord, I don't want to assume that I am doing everything right. I know You allow certain painful things to happen to us when we don't live Your way. If I am going through a difficult time because of something I have done, or something I didn't do that I should have, reveal it to me so that I can confess it to You. I want to repent of it and turn away from doing anything wrong and make things right between us. If I am going through a difficult time that You are allowing for a purpose, I thank You in advance for the good You will bring out of it.

Unto the upright there arises light in the darkness; He is gracious, and full of compassion, and righteous.

PSALM 112:4

When I Need Help in Tough Times

Lord, I cry out to You today and ask You to give me relief from the difficult things I am facing. Bring them to a good conclusion as only You can do. I know You understand all that I am going through, and You see all I do and what I am up against (Psalm 139:2-3). You even know my thoughts about my circumstances right now. Help me to navigate these rough waters so that I can not only survive, but come through victoriously.

In the day when I cried out, You answered me, and made me bold with strength in my soul.

PSALM 138:3

When I Need Help in Tough Times

Dear God, I thank You that the difficult situations in my life will not last forever. I pray You will cause them all to come to a good end and that each outcome will bring glory to You. Help me to not dwell on the problems I see, but to dwell on Your power and mercy, which I may not be able to see at the time, but I know is always there for me. Help me to remember that my problems are temporary, but what You will do in me in the midst of them will last forever.

For our light affliction, which is but for a moment, is working for us a far more exceeding and eternal weight of glory, while we do not look at the things which are seen, but at the things which are not seen. For the things which are seen are temporary, but the things which are not seen are eternal.

2 CORINTHIANS 4:17-18

When I Need Comfort and Guidance

*D*ear Lord, I praise You today and give thanks to You for Your great mercy to me. Thank You that You see the places where I struggle and have given me the presence of Your Holy Spirit to comfort and guide me at all times. I pray for a greater sense of Your comfort and a deeper understanding of the ways You provide Your guidance to me. In the difficult things I face, I don't want to make a move without knowing You are leading me. Help me to not miss Your instructions to my heart.

Sing, O heavens! Be joyful, O earth! And break out in singing, O mountains! For the LORD has comforted His people, and will have mercy on His afflicted.

ISAIAH 49:13

When I Need Comfort and Guidance

*L*ord, I reverence You and fear Your name. For You are the Almighty Creator of all, who created me for a high purpose. Help me to not worry about what anyone says or does to me. Help me to get my eyes off of others and onto You and all that You are. Cover me with Your protective hand and hide me from the dangers that lurk around me. Keep me safe from the plans of evil people. I depend on You to safely guide me where You want me to go.

I, even I, am He who comforts you. Who are you that you should be afraid of a man who will die, and of the son of a man who will be made like grass?

ISAIAH 51:12

When I Need Comfort and Guidance

$\mathcal{T}$hank You, Lord, that You have sent a wonderful guide and Helper—Your Holy Spirit—to live in me. Now when times are difficult, or I face disturbing situations, I can always find my comfort in You. Today I pray that You will give me comfort and peace about the troubling situations in my life. Help me to rely on You only to comfort my soul instead of looking to others and being disappointed. Only Your comfort is lasting and sure.

I will pray the Father, and He will give you another Helper, that He may abide with you forever.

JOHN 14:16

204

When I Need Comfort and Guidance

*D*ear Father in heaven, I thank You that even though I may find myself in a dangerous place sometime, I don't have to fear evil because You are there to protect me. It comforts me to know that You will always lead me and correct my course when I need it. Help me to continually follow Your lead and receive Your correction. Help me to never be careless so I can end up in the wrong place at the wrong time. I depend on You to keep me safe.

Yea, though I walk through the valley of the shadow of death, I will fear no evil; for You are with me; Your rod and Your staff, they comfort me.

PSALM 23:4

When I Need Comfort
and Guidance

Dear Lord, thank You for Your comfort in my life. I draw near to You and seek Your comfort today. Thank You that Your love and comfort is so great that it surrounds me completely, and there is no part of my life that is beyond the reach of Your loving care and healing touch. I ask that You would reach down and touch me with Your healing power and take away any pain I feel, both physically and emotionally. Free me from misery and discomfort and enable me to live a productive life so I can do great things for Your glory.

You shall increase my greatness, and comfort me on every side.

PSALM 71:21

When I Need Comfort and Guidance

*L*ord, I thank You for Your Word that guides me, gives me life, and comforts my soul. When my soul is troubled, afflicted, or afraid, help me to find comfort in Your presence and in Your truth. When I go through things that torment my soul, I pray that the comfort of Your Holy Spirit will ease my pain, and the comfort of Your Word will enlarge my perspective. Help me to get to the point that I seek comfort and guidance from only You and from nothing or no one else.

This is my comfort in my affliction, for Your word has given me life.

PSALM 119:50

When I Need Comfort and Guidance

*L*ord, Your merciful kindness toward me brings me great comfort. Help me to remember that Your love and mercy never fail, especially during the times when it seems as if my prayers have not been answered. Help me to see that even in difficult struggles, You are always on my side. Thank You that You are a good God and the life You have for me is good. Help me to trust that about You at all times, so that I will seek Your comfort and guidance at the first sign of trouble or difficulty.

Let, I pray, Your merciful kindness be for my comfort, according to Your word to Your servant.

PSALM 119:76

When I Need Comfort and Guidance

Thank You, Lord, that You have forgiven me of my sins and my warfare has ended. You have won the victory for me, and now You have a place of rest and comfort for me, no matter where I am in my life. Even though it seems that I have paid a great price for times when I have strayed off the path You have for me, I know Your reward to those who persevere is multiplied. Help me to persevere on Your path for my life and lay claim to the comfort You have for me now.

Speak comfort to Jerusalem, and cry out to her, that her warfare is ended, that her iniquity is pardoned; for she has received from the LORD's hand double for all her sins.

ISAIAH 40:2

When I Need Comfort and Guidance

*D*ear Lord, I want to thank You for all the help and comfort You have given to me in my life. Help me to be able to comfort others who are having problems with that same comfort. Flow *through* me all that You have poured *into* me. If I hesitate to reach out to others for fear of rejection, give me the confidence and understanding I need to know when and how to be Your hand extended.

Blessed be the God and Father of our Lord Jesus Christ, the Father of mercies and God of all comfort, who comforts us in all our tribulation, that we may be able to comfort those who are in any trouble, with the comfort with which we ourselves are comforted by God.

2 Corinthians 1:3-4

When I Need Comfort and Guidance

*L*ord, I need Your guidance in my life right now. I have to make decisions that I don't want to make without knowing Your will for me. Give me wisdom and revelation about these things. Your counsel is great above all others. Your guidance is perfect. I seek Your counsel and guidance today. Fill me with Your wisdom so that when I have to make a quick decision, it will be the right one. I find great comfort in knowing I am in Your perfect will.

This also comes from the LORD of hosts, who is wonderful in counsel and excellent in guidance.

ISAIAH 28:29

When I Need Comfort
and Guidance

*L*ord, I turn to You as the solid rock on which I stand and ask that You would lead me in the way I should go. I seek Your guidance and revelation. I look to You for wisdom and correction. I don't want to take a step without knowing You are leading me. The decisions I need to make must be the right ones, so don't let me make a mistake. Even when I must make a quick decision, help me to do so with great accuracy because of the wisdom and knowledge You have put in me. Make me sensitive to the presence and leading of Your Holy Spirit in my heart.

You are my rock and my fortress; therefore, for Your name's sake, lead me and guide me.

PSALM 31:3

When I Need Comfort and Guidance

*L*ord, I seek Your face right now and ask that as I look to You, You will guide me where I need to go. Your presence comforts me, and the knowledge that I am walking in Your will makes me confident and secure. Help me to stay on the path You have for me. Help me to come to You every day for guidance and not try to do things on my own. Enable me to keep my eyes on You at all times.

I will instruct you and teach you in the way you should go; I will guide you with My eye.

PSALM 32:8

When I Need Comfort and Guidance

*L*ord, I ask that You would restore any place in my life that is like a wasteland. Make the dead places come alive. Take the dry places in me and make them to be like a well-watered garden. In the areas of my life where I don't see much fruit, make the roots of my life go down deep in You. Where I have felt as though I were in a wilderness, transform that part of my life into a lush garden. Put in me a heart of thanksgiving and a voice that will always sing Your praise.

The LORD will comfort Zion, He will comfort all her waste places; He will make her wilderness like Eden, and her desert like the garden of the LORD; joy and gladness will be found in it, thanksgiving and the voice of melody.

ISAIAH 51:3

When I Need Comfort and Guidance

*L*ord, I pray You will guide me continually so that I never get off the path You have for me. And if I have already strayed from Your will in any way, I pray You will give me a convicted heart and the determination I need to get back into the center of Your will right away. In the dryness of my soul, I pray You will comfort and refresh me with Your living water so that it becomes an eternal spring in my heart. Make my soul and my mind to be whole and flourishing.

The LORD will guide you continually, and satisfy your soul in drought, and strengthen your bones; you shall be like a watered garden, and like a spring of water, whose waters do not fail.

ISAIAH 58:11

When I Need Comfort
and Guidance

*L*ord, Your Word says that having integrity will be a guide to me. It will help me make sound moral judgments. I pray that You would help me to be a person of integrity—one who is honest and upright. Help me to be sound and complete. Make me whole so that my wholeness will keep my integrity from ever being compromised. Let my integrity guide me so that I am always able to make the right decision at the right time.

The integrity of the upright will guide them, but the perversity of the unfaithful will destroy them.

PROVERBS 11:3

When I Need Comfort and Guidance

*L*ord, I praise You as the God of all comfort and patience and the Father of all mercy. Today I need Your comfort and mercy in a great way. I come to You to lay the things that trouble my soul at Your feet. Be merciful to me and take them away. Fill me with the comfort of Your love. Thank You, Lord, that You are patient with me when I fail or stray away from Your perfect will for my life. Thank You that You keep watch over me at all times.

May the God of patience and comfort grant you to be like-minded toward one another, according to Christ Jesus.

ROMANS 15:5

When I Need Comfort and Guidance

*L*ord, I look to You for counsel and guidance. Help me to know what to do and when to do it. Show me whenever I need to seek the help of godly counselors who also look to You for counsel. When I need specific knowledge about what to do that I can only get from You and the people You bring into my life for that reason, show me exactly whom to go to for counsel. Guide me every step of the way on my journey through life, and please be there to guide me especially on the day I step into eternity with You.

You will guide me with Your counsel, and afterward receive me to glory.

PSALM 73:24

When I Need a
New Attitude

*D*ear God, I thank You that You make all things new. Thank You that there will be a time when You will make everything so new that there will be no more crying or sorrow, no more pain or death. I pray that today You will make me and my attitude new. Help me to get rid of any mind-set that would keep me from becoming more like You and receiving the blessings You have for me. If I have a negative attitude about anything, help me to throw it off and put on a positive new one. Make me more and more into the image of Christ.

God will wipe away every tear from their eyes; there shall be no more death, nor sorrow, nor crying. There shall be no more pain, for the former things have passed away. Then He who sat on the throne said, "Behold, I make all things new."

REVELATION 21:4-5

When I Need a New Attitude

*D*ear Lord, I pray that You will help me to not grow weary in well doing. Keep me from giving up when times of discouragement happen and it seems as if doing the right thing isn't working. Help me to continue on in what I know of You and Your ways and not take matters into my own hands and try to do things my way. Help me to refuse to be discouraged, for I know by faith that there will be a reaping of good things because I have sowed good seed.

Let us not grow weary while doing good, for in due season we shall reap if we do not lose heart.

GALATIANS 6:9

When I Need a New Attitude

*D*ear God, I pray You would give me a cheerful heart that is reflected in my face, especially when other people see me. Please keep me far from having a heart of sorrow or a broken spirit. Where my heart has been broken in the past, I pray that You would heal it completely. I want to live in Your joy of heart and the wholeness of spirit You have for me. Help me make choices each day to maintain the positive, uplifting, and hopeful attitude I need to have in order to glorify You and see Your will done in my life.

A merry heart makes a cheerful countenance, but by sorrow of the heart the spirit is broken.

PROVERBS 15:13

When I Need a New Attitude

*T*hank You, Lord, for Your grace and for the faith You have given me to be able to receive it. Help me to never forget that Your salvation is a gift to me. I don't want to take this gift for granted. I want to always have humble gratitude to You for saving me from an eternity in hell and from living a life of hell on earth. Help me to never have an arrogant or casual attitude about the blessings You have given me, as if I had done anything to deserve them or earn them. Give me a renewed attitude about that today.

By grace you have been saved through faith, and that not of yourselves; it is the gift of God, not of works, lest anyone should boast.

EPHESIANS 2:8-9

When I Need a New Attitude

*L*ord, I want to make praise to You the first thing I do every day. I want to wake up in the morning with thoughts of You on my mind and with joy in my heart because You are in charge of my life. I want to lay my requests before You, even before I have time to worry about them. Help me do that every day so that anxiety and depression have no place in me. Correct my attitude so that it becomes one of joy-filled hope.

My voice You shall hear in the morning, O LORD; in the morning I will direct it to You, and I will look up.

PSALM 5:3

When I Need a
New Attitude

*L*ord, help me to discern the lies of the enemy so that I don't give any credence to thoughts that are not in alignment with Your truth. Help me to examine my thoughts in light of Your Word at all times. Enable me to purify my thoughts and my heart so that evil will not find a place in me. Adjust my attitude to fit life in Your kingdom. Overflow my heart with Your love, peace, joy, gentleness, kindness, and mercy until my attitude is a blessing to all people at all times.

Examine me, O Lord, and prove me; try my mind and my heart.

Psalm 26:2

When I Need a New Attitude

Dear God, I pray You would cleanse my heart of all that is not of You. Pour out Your Spirit afresh in my life and wash away all negative attitudes and feelings. Renew my soul so that it is steadfast and strong. Purify my heart by pouring into me Your purity and holiness. Align my thoughts with Yours so that the mind of Christ is clearly manifest in me. Create in me a clean heart and renew a right spirit within me so that I can become the whole person You made me to be.

Create in me a clean heart, O God, and renew a steadfast spirit within me.

PSALM 51:10

When I Need a
New Attitude

*L*ord, fill my mind with Your truth and keep me undeceived. Help me to take charge of my thoughts and refuse any that are in opposition to Your ways. Flush out all thoughts that are ungodly or sinful. Help me to keep my heart clean and pure before You at all times so that I can be a vessel prepared for Your service. When my attitude is not glorifying to You, adjust it to Your standards.

I, the Lord, *search the heart, I test the mind, even to give every man according to his ways, according to the fruit of his doings.*

JEREMIAH 17:10

When I Need a New Attitude

$\mathcal{L}$ord, help me to live with truth in my heart and not give place to lies. I want to dwell in Your presence where everything makes sense, and all is truth, and there is always hope. Transform my mind so that I have a new outlook. Take away all negative and unproductive thoughts, and give me a new way of thinking that does not conform to the world. Help me to live in Your perfect will and prove to all who see me that Your way is the right way to live. Enable me to abide with You in a steady, unwavering way.

Lord, who may abide in Your tabernacle? Who may dwell in Your holy hill? He who walks uprightly, and works righteousness, and speaks the truth in his heart.

PSALM 15:1-2

When I Need a New Attitude

*L*ord, help me to have a good, positive, hopeful, joyous, and bright attitude today. Uplift my spirit and fill me afresh with Your joy. May Your joy rise in my heart right now in such abundance that it overflows onto others who see me. And when I speak, may Your Spirit of joy be contagious. I praise Your name and glorify You as the lifter of my head when I am down. You are my everlasting Father, who has given me a wonderful life for all eternity.

Make a joyful shout to the LORD, all you lands! Serve the LORD with gladness; come before His presence with singing.

PSALM 100:1-2

When I Need a
New Attitude

*L*ord, forgive me for any bad or wrong attitude I have had. I confess the times I have sinned in that way. I know that a bad attitude is a sign of a lack of faith in You. It's a lack of trust that You will help me, heal me, or keep me safe. When I start feeling bad because things are not going my way, I will confess that as pride. Purify my heart and help me to not fall into the trap of the enemy by clinging to any attitude that is ungodly or doesn't glorify You—especially in my own home and among my family members.

I will behave wisely in a perfect way. Oh, when will You come to me? I will walk within my house with a perfect heart.

PSALM 101:2

When I Need a New Attitude

$\mathcal{L}$ord, I worship You and bless You with my whole heart and soul. Thank You for all You have done for me. Thank You that because I live for You, You have given me favor in Your eyes and favor with other people. Help me to be a blessing to others everywhere I go. Help me to have contagious peace and hopeful anticipation of what is ahead in life. Lord, You have said in Your Word that "he who gets wisdom loves his own soul; he who keeps understanding will find good" (Proverbs 19:8). I pray that wisdom and understanding will be abundant in my life.

Bless the LORD, O my soul; and all that is within me, bless His holy name!

PSALM 103:1

When I Need
Peace and Contentment

Dear heavenly Father, help me to remember that because of Your love for me, I will always be victorious. I am Your child, and You have taught me to be a winner and a conqueror of all that opposes me. I have victory because I am in Christ. Help me to believe all the good things You say about me so that I can live in peace no matter what is happening in my life or in the world around me. Help me to rest so completely in Your love that I don't fear what could happen in the future.

In all these things we are more than conquerors through Him who loved us.

ROMANS 8:37

When I Need
Peace and Contentment

*L*ord, I ask for Your peace that is beyond all comprehension to invade my heart and my mind right now. Help me to live Your way so that I can walk in an upright manner and find the way of peace You have for me to walk. I confess that even though I know You and love You and believe in You, I still have times when I am robbed of peace by the things I hear and see around me. Sometimes the lack of peace in others makes me less peaceful. Help me to keep my eyes only on You so that I can remain in Your peace.

Mark the blameless man, and observe the upright;
for the future of that man is peace.

PSALM 37:37

When I Need
Peace and Contentment

*D*ear Lord, help me to know Your peace in a deeper way today. When I read Your Word, peace and contentment fill my heart. Help me to know Your Word better every time I read it. Help me to understand the truth that is in the Scriptures so that I will always stand on the solid foundation it gives me. When I read of Your laws, I see that they are good and reliable, and when I live by them, life works. Help me to know Your ways and to follow them so that I will never stumble, fall, or fail.

Great peace have those who love Your law, and nothing causes them to stumble.

PSALM 119:165

When I Need
Peace and Contentment

*L*ord, help me to live Your way by obeying Your laws and doing what You instruct my heart to do. I know that both great peace and a sense of assurance come from living according to Your rules. Help me to be content with where I am right now, knowing that when I walk with You, You are always taking me somewhere. You will not leave me where I am forever. At the same time, Lord, help me to know when and how to step out of where I am and refuse to be content with anything less than what You have for me. Give me peace which passes all understanding as I learn to live Your way.

The work of righteousness will be peace, and the effect of righteousness, quietness and assurance forever.

Isaiah 32:17

When I Need
Peace and Contentment

*L*ord, help me to keep my mind focused on You and not on distressing events around me. Help me to trust You so much that I am not fearful or swayed by my emotions. I want to have such strong faith in You and Your Word that even bad news will not throw me. Help me to not even fear bad news because I know You are in charge of my life and You will walk with me and protect me. Protect the people I love and care about as well. Help them to trust in You and know You in a deeper way as well.

You will keep him in perfect peace, whose mind is stayed on You, because he trusts in You.

ISAIAH 26:3

When I Need
Peace and Contentment

*L*ord, I come to You today and lay my heavy burdens at Your feet. I yoke up with You and thank You that You have promised to carry these burdens for me. Thank You that Your yoke is easy and Your burden is light. Thank You for the peace and rest You have for my soul. Help me to move into that rest. Teach me more about You and Your ways so I can live in Your peace. I know that I can never enjoy the level of wholeness You have for me if I have unrest in my soul.

Come to Me, all you who labor and are heavy laden, and I will give you rest. Take My yoke upon you and learn from Me, for I am gentle and lowly in heart, and you will find rest for your souls. For My yoke is easy and My burden is light.

MATTHEW 11:28-30

When I Need
Peace and Contentment

*D*ear Jesus, I am so glad I have put my faith in You. Thank You that You are always drawing me closer to You and that You never give up on me. Thank You for forgiving me of all my past sin and for continuing to forgive me as I confess my sins to You. Because of that, I know my future is secure not only in this life, but also in eternity with You. Such knowledge gives me great peace. Help me to draw on that knowledge and peace whenever I start to worry about things that are happening—or not happening—in my life.

Having been justified by faith, we have peace with God through our Lord Jesus Christ.

ROMANS 5:1

When I Need
Peace and Contentment

*D*ear Lord, when I become concerned about all that is going on in my life, help me to trust You with my whole heart, knowing You will be with me to guide and help me. When I become frustrated by what is *not* happening in my life, help me to not just depend on my own understanding of the situation, but to be able to see things from Your perspective, knowing that You have my best interests in mind. Thank You that You hear the cries of my heart as I look to You in everything I do. I pray that You will continue to guide me on the path You have for me.

In all your ways acknowledge Him, and He shall direct your paths.

PROVERBS 3:6

When I Need
Peace and Contentment

Dear God, I lift to You the things in my life that try to steal my peace and my rest. I surrender to You the situations I face that I feel I cannot accept. Although I get impatient for these things to change, help me to learn to be content and peaceful in the midst of them because I trust You to do the right thing. I trust that You love me enough to always bring good out of the situation. Help me keep my eyes on You and look ahead to the day when these things will no longer trouble me in any way.

Not that I speak in regard to need, for I have learned in whatever state I am, to be content.

PHILIPPIANS 4:11

When I Need
Peace and Contentment

Dear Lord, there is nothing better than learning to live a godly life by obeying You in all things. And how wonderful is the peace and contentment that comes from it. Help me to always be grateful and content with having the things I need. Help me to not be worried about the things I want but don't have. I put the desires of my heart into Your hands, knowing that You abundantly bless those who love You, and You give Your children the desires of their heart when they are in alignment with Your will.

Godliness with contentment is great gain. For we brought nothing into this world, and it is certain we can carry nothing out. And having food and clothing, with these we shall be content.

1 TIMOTHY 6:6-8

When I Need
Peace and Contentment

*H*eavenly Father, I pray that as Your child I will never grieve or disappoint You. You have given me so much, and You promise to continue supplying all my needs in the future. Help me to never be covetous of what anyone else has. You have promised to never forsake me in my need, and I trust You on that. Help me to learn to trust You so completely that even in times when I become concerned about finances or provision, I will turn to You and determine to walk in peace and be content with all that You provide.

Let your conduct be without covetousness; be content with such things as you have. For He Himself has said, "I will never leave you nor forsake you."

HEBREWS 13:5

When I Need
Peace and Contentment

$\mathscr{D}$ear Lord, I need to have a deeper sense of Your peace in me today. Take away all fear, doubt, and concern from my heart and replace it with the peace that only You can give. Thank You that Your peace will guard my mind so that I won't give place to thoughts that are not beneficial to me. Thank You that Your peace will guard my heart from unproductive emotions and feelings that only serve to shatter my life. Thank You that the depth of Your peace is greater than I can imagine, and when I live in it, it makes me whole.

The peace of God, which surpasses all understanding, will guard your hearts and minds through Christ Jesus.

PHILIPPIANS 4:7

When I Need
Peace and Contentment

*L*ord Jesus, I thank You that You died for me so that I could be close to You forever. You are my God and Lord of my life. Because I have invited You into my heart and received You as my Savior, I can walk close to You and enjoy all the peace You have for me. Help me to always remember that, especially when strife and unrest begin to creep back into my soul. Help me to be mindful that You are my peace, and You have broken down every wall of separation that could ever come between me and Your presence.

Now in Christ Jesus you who once were far off have been brought near by the blood of Christ. For He Himself is our peace, who has made both one, and has broken down the middle wall of separation.

EPHESIANS 2:13-14

When I Need
Peace and Contentment

*L*ord, I ask for Your protection upon my home and my surroundings. Thank You that because I have proclaimed You to be Lord over every area of my life and I choose to live Your way every day, I can rest in peace knowing You will keep me secure. Thank You for giving me a quiet and peaceful resting place and home. When my home is not peaceful, I pray that Your Spirit of peace would dwell there and bring peace to all who enter in. Thank You for the wholeness that is worked in my mind, body, and soul because of having a home without strife.

My people will dwell in a peaceful habitation, in secure dwellings, and in quiet resting places.

ISAIAH 32:18

When I Need More Love in My Life

*H*eavenly Father, I thank You that I am Your child and that You love me. Help me to never doubt Your love for me. Help me to trust Your love for me so much that I never even feel a lack of love in my life from anyone else, either in my past, present, or future. Lord, I release anyone in my life who did not love me the way I hoped they would, or did not love me the way I wanted them to. Your love is greater than human love, and it never fails.

Behold what manner of love the Father has bestowed on us, that we should be called children of God! Therefore the world does not know us, because it did not know Him.

1 JOHN 3:1

When I Need More Love in My Life

$Lord$, I open my heart to receive Your perfect love into my mind, emotions, soul, and spirit. Help me to understand the depths of Your love at all times. Jesus, I know You are the Son of God, and because I have received You into my heart, You live in me and Your love dwells in me. Help me to live in Your love and not doubt it. Help me to grow more and more secure in Your love so that I can grow and thrive the way a child does with a loving parent.

Whoever confesses that Jesus is the Son of God, God abides in him, and he in God. And we have known and believed the love that God has for us. God is love, and he who abides in love abides in God, and God in him.

1 JOHN 4:15-16

When I Need More Love in My Life

Lord, I know that to put my life in proper order, I need to love You above all things and all people. Show me where I am not loving You with all my heart, soul, and mind. Reveal to me where I have a divided heart, and I will turn away from whatever divides my attention and draws me away from You. Show me what it means to love You with everything I have in me.

Jesus said to him, "You shall love the LORD your God with all your heart, with all your soul, and with all your mind." This is the first and great commandment.

MATTHEW 22:37-38

When I Need More Love in My Life

*L*ord, there are some days when I feel unloved, and that can cause me to feel unloving. I confess both these feelings to You as sin. Your Word says You love me, and all I know of You speaks of Your love for me. You saved me because You love me. You deliver me because You love me. You provide for me because You love me. Help me to trust Your love at all times. Help me to be free of any feelings of being unloved because in You I have enough love to heal me to complete wholeness.

Let us who are of the day be sober, putting on the breastplate of faith and love, and as a helmet the hope of salvation.

1 Thessalonians 5:8

When I Need More Love in My Life

$\mathcal{T}$hank You, Lord, that there is nothing that can separate me from Your love. There is no place I can go that will cause me to be lost from You. If I go to the greatest depth, You see me. If I travel to the most remote place on earth, Your love still finds me. Jesus, even when all deserted You, You were never alone because God was with You. Help me to sense Your holy presence in that same way in my life.

Indeed the hour is coming, yes, has now come, that you will be scattered, each to his own, and will leave Me alone. And yet I am not alone, because the Father is with Me.

John 16:32

When I Need More
Love in My Life

$Lord$, fill me with Your love so that it overflows from me to others. Help me to not have a critical spirit so that I become cynical and lose my joy. Help me to not be a complainer, but instead to see Your good in every situation. Teach me how to love the way You do. I know that nothing I accomplish on earth will have any lasting value unless I walk with love in my heart for You, Lord, and for others as well.

Though I have the gift of prophecy, and under-stand all mysteries and all knowledge, and though I have all faith, so that I could remove mountains, but have not love, I am nothing.

1 CORINTHIANS 13:2

When I Need More Love in My Life

$\mathcal{L}$ord, I worship You and thank You that You are a God of love. Fill me with Your love today. Pour out Your love in my heart right now as I praise You. Because I love You so much, I want to keep Your Word and obey You. Enable me to live Your way so that I never minimize Your presence in my life. I invite You to make Your home with me today and every day.

Jesus answered and said to him, "If anyone loves Me, he will keep My word; and My Father will love him, and We will come to him and make our home with him."

JOHN 14:23

When I Need More Love in My Life

Thank You, Lord, for loving me as I am. Thank You for loving me enough to not leave me the way I am, but rather You have chosen to lead me into a life of wholeness. Help me to live in Your love. Help me to understand who You made me to be so that I can move into all You have for me. I know that emotional healing can only happen in the presence of unconditional love. And Your love is the only love powerful and complete enough to love me to wholeness.

As the Father loved Me, I also have loved you; abide in My love.

JOHN 15:9

When I Need More Love in My Life

$\mathcal{L}$ord, knowing that You love me gives me great peace. Help me to love You with a pure heart, so that no part of me loves something or someone else more than I love You. Help me to have love in my heart even when I have to confront difficult and trying things. I pray that Your love will perfect me and bring wholeness to my relationships and situations.

Let the peace of God rule in your hearts, to which also you were called in one body; and be thankful.

COLOSSIANS 3:15

When I Need More Love in My Life

*D*ear God, I thank You that before I ever knew You, You loved me enough to send Your Son to die for me so I wouldn't have to pay the price for my own sins. Love so great as that is unfathomable. Help me to love others the way You love me. Help me to sacrifice something of myself in order to show love to the people around me. I know that in order to be loved by others, I must show love to them. Enable me to do that in a way that can be perceived.

In this is love, not that we loved God, but that He loved us and sent His Son to be the propitiation for our sins. Beloved, if God so loved us, we also ought to love one another.

1 JOHN 4:10-11

When I Need More Love in My Life

*L*ord, I want to fully understand and sense the depth of Your love for me. Fill me with Your love today so that it overflows to others. I know that godly love is greater than even the strength of faith and hope. May the fullness of Your love in my life bring healing and wholeness to the parts of me that are unloving or unlovable. Where I have felt unloved, I pray You would heal that wound. Free me to love others the way that You do.

Now abide faith, hope, love, these three; but the greatest of these is love.

1 CORINTHIANS 13:13

When I Need More Love in My Life

*L*ord, I thank You that You love and care about me enough to know me well. You know where I go and what I do. You know all about me, and You still love me. God, I pray I would sense Your amazing love—especially when I don't feel known or loved by others. Whenever I am in a place or social situation where I know no one, help me to sense Your love and connection to me in a deeper way than ever.

You know my sitting down and my rising up; You understand my thought afar off. You comprehend my path and my lying down, and are acquainted with all my ways.

PSALM 139:2-3

When I Need Greater Faith

*L*ord, I ask that You would give me greater faith. Help me to trust You for the things I can't see. Help me to believe You for the things I hope for. I thank You in advance for hearing and answering my prayers, even though I may not see those answers manifest for some time. Help me to not lose hope when the answer to my prayers is delayed. Help me to grow ever stronger in faith as I wait on You. Thank You for my healing and wholeness that is yet to come.

Now faith is the substance of things hoped for, the evidence of things not seen.

HEBREWS 11:1

When I Need Greater Faith

*L*ord, I worship You and give You the glory due Your name. I worship You in the beauty of Your holiness. I thank You that as I praise You, You are bringing my life into alignment with Your purposes. Help me to sing Your praises even when I wake up troubled in the night. Even when my soul is heavy and I don't feel like singing at all, I pray that You would put a song in my heart that rises out of me and sends away the dark clouds. Help me to know Your Word so well that I can sing of it in my praise to You.

Let the saints be joyful in glory; let them sing aloud on their beds. Let the high praises of God be in their mouth, and a two-edged sword in their hand.

PSALM 149:5-6

When I Need Greater Faith

*L*ord, I pray You would take away all fear of failure from me. Take away any plaguing doubt that says I can never be good enough to do things right. When I hear the voice of the enemy telling me that what You have made me to be is not enough, help me to resist him with Your truth. Take away any nagging doubts and fears I have that I will eventually do something terribly wrong and suffer because of it. Help me to rely on You in greater faith and not be tossed up and down like a ship in a storm. Thank You that You are my anchor in all kinds of weather.

Let him ask in faith, with no doubting, for he who doubts is like a wave of the sea driven and tossed by the wind.

JAMES 1:6

When I Need Greater Faith

*L*ord, help me to have the kind of powerful faith that doesn't give way to doubt when things appear to go wrong. I have faith in You and that You are a good God. I have faith in Your love for me. I have faith that You are the God of the impossible. Help me to believe that You will do the impossible in my life. Help me to have faith every time I pray, that You will hear my prayer and that You will answer it in Your perfect timing and according to Your perfect will for my life.

Immediately the father of the child cried out and said with tears, "Lord, I believe; help my unbelief!"

MARK 9:24

When I Need
Greater Faith

Lord, You have said that the just shall live by faith. Help me to always live by faith in You, Your power, and Your ability to do the impossible. Help me to continue to have faith that Your love for me will never fail. Help me to not fall into the prideful attitude of having faith in my own ability to make things happen. Keep my soul upright within me and correct my mind and heart if I don't rely on Your unfailing hand of grace.

Behold the proud, His soul is not upright in him;
but the just shall live by his faith.

HABAKKUK 2:4

When I Need Greater Faith

*L*ord, I ask You to give me faith that is strong enough to believe for healing for my body and soul when I pray for it. Help me to be like the woman who, in Your Word, You told that her faith had made her well. Lord give me that kind of strong faith—the faith I need in order to believe for Your healing touch in my body and soul. Take away all doubt and reveal anything in me that would keep me from experiencing total healing.

He said to her, "Daughter, your faith has made you well. Go in peace, and be healed of your affliction."

MARK 5:34

When I Need
Greater Faith

*L*ord, in Your Word You said to the two blind men seeking healing, "According to your faith, let it be to you." And You healed them because they believed You could. Your words are sobering and make me evaluate my own faith. I need healing too. I need my eyes to be opened to see what I need to see. I also need greater faith to believe that You can and will do such great things in my life. I am also sobered by the possibility that my own *insufficient* faith may be hindering the healing I need. Strengthen my faith, O Lord, to believe for the total healing and wholeness You have for me.

He touched their eyes, saying, "According to your faith let it be to you."

MATTHEW 9:29

When I Need
Greater Faith

*L*ord, sometimes I feel as though I'm falling. I try to walk above the things that threaten to wash over me, but I often feel as though I will be sucked under. I pray that if I start to fall, You will reach out, catch me, and lift me up. Most of all, I pray that my faith will be so strong that You won't ever think of me as having little faith. Give me big faith to believe for the big things You want to do in my life.

Immediately Jesus stretched out His hand and caught him, and said to him, "O you of little faith, why did you doubt?"

MATTHEW 14:31

When I Need
Greater Faith

*D*ear Lord, one of my greatest desires is to be able to pray for others and see them healed. I pray that You would grow in me the kind of faith that is great enough to do something so wonderful for people who are suffering and have no hope. You are a healer, and in Your Word You made the connection between faith and healing. Give me faith to believe not only for healing for myself, but for the healing of others every time I pray for them.

Jesus answered and said to her, "O woman, great is your faith! Let it be to you as you desire." And her daughter was healed from that very hour.

MATTHEW 15:28

When I Need Greater Faith

*L*ord, I need mountain-moving faith today because there are situations in my life that loom large like mountains and I can't begin to move them. But I believe in You and Your power on my behalf. Surely my faith is as big as a mustard seed. Take what faith I have and grow it into a giant tree of faith so that I can speak to the mountain-sized obstacles in my life and see them moved. Thank You, Lord, that with You, nothing is impossible.

Jesus said to them, "Because of your unbelief; for assuredly, I say to you, if you have faith as a mustard seed, you will say to this mountain, 'Move from here to there,' and it will move; and nothing will be impossible for you."

MATTHEW 17:20

When I Need
Greater Faith

*L*ord, I confess that I sometimes fear my needs won't be met. I worry that something will happen and there won't be enough. Lord, give me faith to believe that You will always enable me to have what I need. Take away all fear in me about Your desire to provide for me and replace it with deeper faith in You and Your great power on my behalf. Grow my faith to believe for things that are greater than I can even imagine right now.

If then God so clothes the grass, which today is in the field and tomorrow is thrown into the oven, how much more will He clothe you, O you of little faith?

LUKE 12:28

When I Need
Greater Faith

*D*ear Lord, I pray as Your own apostles did, that You would increase my faith. If those who saw You every day and witnessed Your awesome works needed to ask for greater faith, how much more do I? If they who witnessed Your wonders and miracles still struggled with doubt, how great must my own doubt be? I don't want to limit what You want to do in my life because of doubt, so I pray that You would make my faith big enough to facilitate all You want to do *in* me and *through* me. Give me faith to believe for the complete wholeness You want to work in my life.

The apostles said to the Lord, "Increase our faith."

LUKE 17:5

When I Need Greater Faith

*L*ord, I need the faith to believe that I can be victorious over everything that opposes me. Give me faith that does not fear death at all because I know that You will be the first face I see in heaven. Help me to believe without doubt that You are my healer and deliverer. Help me to have faith that You will never leave me or forsake me. My faith in You has saved me for eternity. May my faith in You be big enough to save me from myself now.

He said to the woman, "Your faith has saved you. Go in peace."

LUKE 7:50

When I Need Greater Faith

$\mathcal{L}$ord, I know You have called those of us who are Your sons and daughters to have faith in You and in Your ability to keep us and guide us. Help me to do that. Help me to make faith a daily walk. Help me to learn to live by faith in all that I do and to trust You for each day and all that is in it. I know my brokenness cannot be mended without faith in Your ability and desire to do it. I trust You to do whatever is necessary to bring me to complete wholeness.

I am not ashamed of the gospel of Christ, for it is the power of God to salvation for everyone who believes, for the Jew first and also for the Greek. For in it the righteousness of God is revealed from faith to faith; as it is written, "The just shall live by faith."

ROMANS 1:16-17

When I Need Greater Faith

Lord, I feel as if my faith is tested every day. Help me to pass those tests so that my faith will be strengthened and shine as pure gold. Help my faith to remain strong, steadfast, and unwavering so that my actions will glorify You in the sight of others. I pray that every trial I go through will make my trust in You and Your Word grow stronger and stronger.

In this you greatly rejoice, though now for a little while, if need be, you have been grieved by various trials, that the genuineness of your faith, being much more precious than gold that perishes, though it is tested by fire, may be found to praise, honor, and glory at the revelation of Jesus Christ.

1 PETER 1:6-7

When I Need Greater Faith

$\mathcal{L}$ord, help me to pray with great faith for my own healing and for others who are sick and want to be healed as well. You have said that the prayers of faith will save the sick and You will raise him up. You are my healer, and I pray that my faith in Your ability and desire to heal would grow bigger with every passing day. One of the greatest dreams I have is to pray for people to be healed and to see You heal them. Please give me that desire of my heart. Answer my prayers for healing when I pray in faith to You.

The prayer of faith will save the sick, and the Lord will raise him up. And if he has committed sins, he will be forgiven.

JAMES 5:15

When I Need
Greater Faith

*L*ord, I know that faith alone is not enough, but I also have to act on my faith. Help me to step out and behave as though I believe what I say I believe. Even now I rejoice over the things I am trusting You to do in my life. I have faith in Your Word; help me to take action on what You teach me in it. I choose to believe that You always hear my prayers and will answer them. Help me to act on that faith by not growing anxious about how everything is going to turn out in my life.

You see then that a man is justified by works, and not by faith only.

JAMES 2:24

When I Need Greater Faith

*L*ord, I put my faith in You and not in others. I know the wisdom of man is nothing compared to Your wisdom. I put my faith in Your power and not the might of mere men. For no power is greater than Yours. No one else can do the impossible in my life but You. There are many situations in which I am depending on You to do the impossible to fix things or else to transform my circumstances. Grow my faith to trust that until it's time to go to be with You in eternity, You will take care of me here on earth.

Your faith should not be in the wisdom of men but in the power of God.

1 Corinthians 2:5

When I Need Greater Faith

*L*ord, help me to walk by faith and not be brought down by doubt because of situations I see around me. Help me to refuse to let what appears to be happening to distress me and cause me to doubt. Enable me to get my eyes off the things that make me afraid and put them on You instead. I want to walk by faith every single day. Help me to get up each morning and say, "I walk in faith this day through every challenge." Help me to pray about everything and then, once I have prayed, to leave the answer to that prayer in Your hands.

We walk by faith, not by sight.

2 Corinthians 5:7

When I Need
Greater Faith

*L*ord, I thank You that my faith is increased every time I read Your Word. I pray it will increase every time I speak Your Word or even think on Your Word. When I read the Bible, help me to understand what I have read and apply it to my life. Help me to act on what it is instructing me to do. Help me to learn it and memorize it. And every time I read it or quote it, increase my faith. Give me strong faith in You, Your promises, and Your Word. Engrave Your Word on my heart so that my faith is always increasing.

Faith comes by hearing, and hearing by the word of God.

ROMANS 10:17

When I Need
to Speak Life

*G*od, I pray that You would cause only good and excellent things to come from my lips. Fill my heart with Your love, peace, patience, and kindness so that it overflows from my mouth. Help me to speak of positive things and not negative—words that bring life and not death. I know the words I speak can bring blessings into my life or they can keep blessings from me. Help me to never shut off the flow of all You have for me by speaking words that are not glorifying to You.

Listen, for I will speak of excellent things, and from the opening of my lips will come right things.

PROVERBS 8:6

When I Need
to Speak Life

$\mathscr{L}$ord, I pray You would give me the ability to always speak the right words at the right time. Make me to be like the most educated scholar so that I am easily able to choose words that heal, calm, edify, and uplift the people I talk to. Help me to get outside of myself and be focused entirely on those who need the kind of comfort and encouragement a timely word can bring. Enable me to have the perfect words for each situation and need.

The Lord GOD *has given Me the tongue of the learned, that I should know how to speak a word in season to him who is weary.*

ISAIAH 50:4

278

When I Need
to Speak Life

Lord, I know that, as Your child, the words I speak should represent You well. I pray that my heart will be so full of Your Spirit that I will only speak the words You give me to say. May the words I speak lay a foundation of Your love and purpose in the lives of others. Help me to never speak words that bring destruction, either to me or to anyone else. I know that what I say can bring life not only to other people, but also life to me as well.

I have put My words in your mouth; I have covered you with the shadow of My hand, that I may plant the heavens, lay the foundations of the earth, and say to Zion, "You are My people."

ISAIAH 51:16

When I Need to Speak Life

*L*ord, I know that whatever is in my heart will eventually be revealed in what I say. If my heart is full of bitterness, jealousy, or anger, it will come out in a moment of weakness and bring destruction and hurt to others. So I pray that You would create in me a clean heart and fill my heart with Your love, joy, and peace. May my heart be so full of Your Spirit, that what flows out of my mouth are only godly, Spirit-filled, and anointed words that bring life to all who hear me.

Brood of vipers! How can you, being evil, speak good things? For out of the abundance of the heart the mouth speaks.

MATTHEW 12:34

When I Need
to Speak Life

*L*ord, I pray You would give me the perfect words to say every time I am called upon to speak—either one-on-one, in casual conversation, or in front of a group of people. I don't want to always be worried about what to say or feel concerned because I am afraid I didn't say the right thing or feel terrible because I said the wrong thing. Lord, I know from Your Word that You can give me words to say and the perfect timing as to when to say them. I pray You would give me that ability always.

When they deliver you up, do not worry about how or what you should speak. For it will be given to you in that hour what you should speak.

MATTHEW 10:19

When I Need to Speak Life

Lord, help me to guard my mouth so that I won't speak careless or destructive words. I regret any time I have said words that may have hurt someone or made them feel bad. Help me to be careful with the words I speak so that they always bring life, love, and encouragement to others. Enable me to do that so I can keep my own soul from trouble. I know that the words I speak can set the stage in my life for the good or the bad. Help me to speak words that build up and not tear down.

Whoever guards his mouth and tongue keeps his soul from troubles.

PROVERBS 21:23

When I Need to Speak Life

Lord, help me to always know when to speak and when to keep silent. Help me to not reveal secrets that others expect me to keep private. Keep a guard over my mouth so that I will not be a talebearer who violates a confidence, but rather help me to be a faithful and discreet person who has the ability to keep things concealed. Help me to not be a person whose mouth is always running and who doesn't listen. Make me a person with a faithful spirit who can listen carefully and speak with discretion.

A talebearer reveals secrets, but he who is of a faithful spirit conceals a matter.

PROVERBS 11:13

When I Need
to Speak Life

*L*ord, help me to not bring condemnation into my life by the words I speak. I don't want to bring judgment upon myself by foolish or careless things I say. Instead, help me to speak words that bring salvation, love, and gladness to others. Teach me to speak positive words about myself and my own life as well. Help me to never speak words that are not glorifying to You or that grieve Your Spirit. Put a guard over my heart and mouth so that my words bring life to me and to others who hear me.

By your words you will be justified, and by your words you will be condemned.

MATTHEW 12:37

When I Need
to Speak Life

*L*ord, help me to not speak ill of anyone or complain about them. I know that such an action will be severely judged and I will be condemned for it. I don't want to shut off the blessings You have for me because I am critical in my thinking or speaking of others. Holy Spirit, strike my heart with conviction if I ever begin to say something about someone that would put them in a negative light. Help me to see the good in everyone and speak words that bring out the best in them.

Do not grumble against one another, brethren, lest you be condemned. Behold, the Judge is standing at the door!

JAMES 5:9

When I Need
to Speak Life

Lord, help me to guard my mouth so that I will not sin when I speak. Help me to always speak the truth from a heart of love that is filled with Your Spirit. I want to walk with You so closely that I hear Your voice telling me what to say and when to say it. Help me, especially, to never speak words that in any way belittle a person in the eyes of another. Keep me from ever saying anything that would bring grief to You.

I said, "I will guard my ways, lest I sin with my tongue; I will restrain my mouth with a muzzle, while the wicked are before me."

PSALM 39:1

When I Need to Speak Life

*L*ord, help me to never speak blasphemy of any kind. I pray, especially, that I will never utter words that blaspheme You or Your Holy Spirit. It is not in my heart to do so, and it grieves me to think that I would. No one could possibly know You, Holy Spirit, and say anything against You, except someone who is hopelessly led by their own lusts. Help me to only speak words of love, blessing, and praise to You or about You all the days of my life.

Anyone who speaks a word against the Son of Man, it will be forgiven him; but whoever speaks against the Holy Spirit, it will not be forgiven him, either in this age or in the age to come.

MATTHEW 12:32

When I Need
to Speak Life

$\mathcal{L}$ord, I know I can't have the wholeness and blessings in my life that You have for me if I don't watch carefully what I say. For I know that with my words I can bring a blessing or a curse upon myself. Take away any negative and destructive thoughts and feelings that I have so that they don't come out in my speech. Remove all critical or judgmental attitudes and any pride that is in me so that I will not bear the consequences of speaking words that reflect those attitudes. Help me to preserve my life with the words I say.

He who guards his mouth preserves his life, but he who opens wide his lips shall have destruction.

PROVERBS 13:3

When I Need to Speak Life

*L*ord, Your Word says that it is not what goes in my mouth that defiles me, but what comes out of it. I pray that I will not undermine all You want to do in my life, and the wholeness You are working in me, by allowing words to come out of my mouth that are not clean, pure, uplifting, and edifying. Correct anything in my heart that is not right so that it will not be reflected in my speech. Help me to always speak words of life, love, and encouragement.

Not what goes into the mouth defiles a man; but what comes out of the mouth, this defiles a man.

MATTHEW 15:11

When I Need
to Speak Life

*D*ear Lord, give me a heart so full of Your love and peace that I only speak words that bring life and not death to the people and situations I am addressing. Let the words of my mouth always be wise and fair. May Your laws and commandments be so engraved on my heart that goodness and righteousness are the fruit of my lips. I know that I will always be on solid ground with You, and I will not get off the path You have for me, if I live Your way. Help me to carefully guard the words I speak so that they always glorify You.

Death and life are in the power of the tongue,
and those who love it will eat its fruit.

PROVERBS 18:21

When I Need to Stand Strong in Times of Weakness

*D*ear Lord, I pray that every day I walk with You, I will grow stronger and stronger. Because I depend on You, I know it is Your strength and not mine that will enable me to do what I otherwise could not. In every place where I feel weak, I declare that I am strong because You, Lord, the Almighty God of the universe, are on my side. Thank You for sharing Your unlimited power with me. Thank You for blessing me in my weakness with Your great strength. Show Your power and strength in me today.

Let the weak say, "I am strong."

JOEL 3:10

When I Need to Stand Strong in Times of Weakness

*D*ear God, I thank You that You give me the strength I need to live through each day and to face all that I must face. The greatest thing I face today is nothing in light of Your ability to do miracles in it. Strengthen me by the power of Your Spirit to stand strong and courageous in the midst of intimidating situations. Give me the power to rise above all opposition and any fear I have as I look toward the challenges in my life right now. Thank You that I can do all things through Christ who strengthens me.

I can do all things through Christ who strengthens me.

PHILIPPIANS 4:13

When I Need to Stand Strong in Times of Weakness

*L*ord, I thank You that in my weakness You empower me. Thank You that You share Your power with whom You love, and I know that I am one of Your beloved children. Because of that, I don't have to be afraid of the times when I feel weak. In fact, when I feel weakest is when You will show Yourself strongest on my behalf. As I draw on Your power and strength today and move forward to fearlessly do Your will, help me to stand strong in all I know of You.

Be strong in the Lord and in the power of His might.

Ephesians 6:10

When I Need to Stand Strong in Times of Weakness

*L*ord, help me to stand especially strong when my prayers have not been answered. Help me to not lose heart, but rather to continue to grow in faith. I have entered the narrow gate by receiving You, but I need Your help to stay on the narrow path of life You have for me. Help me to stand against all temptation to disobey You. Enable me to be one of the few who finds all that You have for those who follow after You.

Narrow is the gate and difficult is the way which leads to life, and there are few who find it.

MATTHEW 7:14

When I Need to Stand Strong in Times of Weakness

*L*ord, when my world is shaken, help me to remember that You are unshakeable. When I feel weak, help me sense Your strength giving me power to rise above my circumstances. When I am afraid, help me to remember to worship You in the face of fear. When I need to stand strong against overpowering challenges, help me to remember all the great things You have already done for me. May those memories increase my faith and give me courage to move ahead. May they provoke wholehearted praise for what You are about to do in my life.

Fear the Lord, *and serve Him in truth with all your heart; for consider what great things He has done for you.*

1 Samuel 12:24

When I Need to Stand
Strong in Times of Weakness

*L*ord, I confess my weaknesses to You, not as sin, but as part of a full acknowledgment of my need for Your power in my life. When I am weak, I pray You will be strong in me. Strengthen me by the power of Your Holy Spirit. Help me to depend on Your strength and not my own. Help me to stand strong in Your power and not my own effort. In the days ahead I will not try to make things happen but will depend on Your Spirit to bring all situations in my life to the perfect conclusion.

He answered and said to me: "This is the word of the LORD to Zerubbabel: 'Not by might nor by power, but by My Spirit,' says the LORD of hosts."

ZECHARIAH 4:6

When I Need to Stand Strong in Times of Weakness

$\mathscr{L}$ord, help me to put on the whole armor You have provided for me so that I can stand strong against the enemy. Help me to be strong in Your Word and in obedience to Your ways. Help me to be steadfast in faith so that I won't waver in the face of ominous circumstances. Help me to be mighty in praise and worship of You, of who You are and all that You do. Help me to be strong in Your power.

Put on the whole armor of God, that you may be able to stand against the wiles of the devil.

Ephesians 6:11

When I Need to Stand Strong in Times of Weakness

*L*ord, when I feel weak I turn to You, for You are my strength. When I am at my weakest, You give me a song in my heart. It's a song of praise to You that I can sing whenever fear threatens to overtake me. Because You have saved me and rescued me from a life of wandering and death, I can now depend on You for guidance, deliverance, healing, and strength. Help me to remember that You are my stronghold in the time of trouble and the rock on which I stand every day.

The LORD is my strength and song, and He has become my salvation. The voice of rejoicing and salvation is in the tents of the righteous; the right hand of the LORD does valiantly.

PSALM 118:14-15

When I Need to Stand Strong in Times of Weakness

*T*hank You, Lord, that in my weakness You are strong. Please perfect Your strength and power in me. In the areas where I feel weakest, I pray that Your strength will be revealed in me as a force to be acknowledged. I know that the things You have called me to do, even in the daily requirements of my life, are things I cannot do without You. Strengthen me to run the race every day with high hopes of great victory.

He said to me, "My grace is sufficient for you, for My strength is made perfect in weakness." Therefore most gladly I will rather boast in my infirmities, that the power of Christ may rest upon me.

2 Corinthians 12:9

When I Need to Stand Strong in Times of Weakness

Lord, I come to You right now to draw on Your strength and power. I ask You to be with me to strengthen me in all areas where I feel weak. I pray that You will help me to stand strong, no matter what comes against me. Save me from the things that would try to destroy me. Your power is far greater than that which I fear could crush me. Thank You that because I draw close to You constantly, You are always near me to be my strength.

You, O Lord, do not be far from Me; O My Strength, hasten to help Me!

PSALM 22:19

When I Need to Stand Strong in Times of Weakness

*L*ord, help me to be strong in You. Forgive me if I have ever been hesitant to publicly say that You are my Lord and I believe in You for fear of the criticism or judgment of others. Help me to stand strong in the midst of opposition or discrimination of any kind. Protect me from gossip or disgrace. Keep my reputation safe from the criticism of those who may want to ruin it. Thank You that I am Your child, and I don't need to be ashamed of anything that happens in my life, for You are either bringing restoration to that area or have allowed it for a great purpose that will be revealed.

The Lord God will help Me; therefore I will not be disgraced; therefore I have set My face like a flint, and I know that I will not be ashamed.

Isaiah 50:7

When I Need to Stand Strong in Times of Weakness

*L*ord, I draw close to You to dwell in Your presence. I can't face all that is ahead of me unless You are with me to give me strength. You are my help in time of need, and You are my shield in the midst of the battle. I need Your strength and power in my life today to sustain me and keep me standing strong. I confess that sometimes I feel too weak to do what You have called me to do— even in my everyday life. Thank You for helping me to stand strong at all times.

Our soul waits for the LORD; He is our help and our shield.

PSALM 33:20

When I Need to Stand Strong in Times of Weakness

Lord, help me to be watchful in prayer. Help me to be so strong in faith that nothing shakes me and I can stand securely through anything. Help me to have the courage to face my challenges and not want to run and hide. Help me to be solid in the things I know about You and diligent to know You more each day. Enable me to never give in to weakness in the way that I live and conduct my life. Let Your power and strength be revealed in me more and more each day.

Watch, stand fast in the faith, be brave, be strong.

1 CORINTHIANS 16:13

When I Need to Stand Strong in Times of Weakness

*L*ord, when I feel weak, help me to remember that You are strong. Help me to rely on Your strength and not doubt it, no matter what is happening. I wait on Your strength to renew me so I can rise up above the things that threaten to overpower my life. The challenges I face are too much for me, and I would be weak just thinking of them if it weren't for my faith in You and Your promises to me.

He gives power to the weak, and to those who have no might He increases strength. Even the youths shall faint and be weary, and the young men shall utterly fall, but those who wait on the LORD shall renew their strength; they shall mount up with wings like eagles, they shall run and not be weary, they shall walk and not faint.

ISAIAH 40:29-31

When I Need to Stand Strong in Times of Weakness

ord, I look to You to strengthen me today. In myself I feel too weak to face the trials and challenges in my life, but in You I have a fortress in which to dwell that cannot be moved or penetrated. You gird me up and lift me above the shaking ground to a place that is solid like a rock. I invite You to display Your strength in me right now and give me peace beyond all imagination. The knowledge of Your power on my behalf gives me great joy.

The LORD will give strength to His people; the LORD will bless His people with peace.

PSALM 29:11

When I Need to Stand Strong in Times of Weakness

Lord, I thank You that I can always see Your goodness in my life, and I know I will continue to see it in the future. Even when I lose hope and can't find joy in my heart, I can live by faith that my hope is in You, and Your joy shall once again rise in my soul. And it will happen this side of heaven. When I have trouble standing strong in certain difficult situations, help me to not lose heart and fall into discouragement. I ask that You would be my strength. Infuse me with Your power so that I become emboldened and invincible.

I would have lost heart, unless I had believed that
I would see the goodness of the LORD *in the land*
of the living.

PSALM 27:13

When I Need to Stand Strong in Times of Weakness

*L*ord, I wait on You because You are my Lord and I trust that You know the very best time to fulfill Your promises to me. I depend on You at all times, but especially when I feel weak in the face of unanswered prayers and postponed dreams. Give me the faith and patience I need to rest in Your timing. You are my strength, and I ask that You would enable me to be strong and whole in my mind, body, and soul as I wait on You to move on my behalf.

Wait on the LORD; *be of good courage, and He shall strengthen your heart; wait, I say, on the* LORD!

PSALM 27:14

When I Need to Stand Strong in Times of Weakness

*D*ear Lord, I praise You as my all-powerful, all-knowing Almighty God. You are my shield when I feel vulnerable. You are my protection when I feel threatened. You are my rock when I feel as though I'm on shaky ground. I rely on You to keep me steady. Help me to lean on only You when I need to stand strong and resist the temptation to lean on something or someone else. I will lift up praise to You whenever I feel weak, rejoicing that I have found my strength in You.

The LORD is my strength and my shield; my heart trusted in Him, and I am helped; therefore my heart greatly rejoices, and with my song I will praise Him.

PSALM 28:7

When I Need to Remember Who I Am in Christ

*T*hank You, Lord, that I am a new creation in Christ, and all the things of the past are far behind me now. Because You have made *all* things new, that means all the old in my life has passed away. I don't have to be chained any longer to old mind-sets, old attitudes, or old ways of doing things that don't work. I don't have to be held back by old limitations. Help me to remember that I am a new creation in every way and to live like it. Help me to remember that You see me through my future and not through my past.

Therefore, if anyone is in Christ, he is a new creation; old things have passed away; behold, all things have become new.

2 Corinthians 5:17

When I Need to Remember Who I Am in Christ

*D*ear Lord, I thank You that You chose me to be Your child. Thank You that You have adopted me into Your family and You are my heavenly Father. Help me to remember Your Father's love for me at all times. Because of You, Jesus, I can be holy and without blame before You—something I could never have accomplished in a lifetime of trying to do right. Help me to remember and understand who I am in Christ.

Just as He chose us in Him before the foundation of the world, that we should be holy and without blame before Him in love, having predestined us to adoption as sons by Jesus Christ to Himself, according to the good pleasure of His will.

EPHESIANS 1:4-5

When I Need to Remember Who I Am in Christ

*D*ear God, I thank You that because I love You and have made You Lord over my life, You are my heavenly Father and I am an heir of Your kingdom. Thank You that even though I am needy in spirit without You, I am rich and prosperous in my soul because of all You have done for me. Thank You that though I was poor in spirit, You have chosen me to be rich in faith. Help me to always remember that I am Your child and I have a rich inheritance in You, both now and for eternity.

Has God not chosen the poor of this world to be rich in faith and heirs of the kingdom which He promised to those who love Him?

JAMES 2:5

When I Need to Remember Who I Am in Christ

*T*hank You, Lord, that You are a God who keeps His promises. They never fail, and I am Your servant for whom Your promises are intended. I reach out today to receive from You all that You have for my life, and I ask that all Your promises will be fulfilled in me. Cleanse me from any lust of the flesh or desire or goal that is not Your best for my life. Cleanse me from anything that keeps me from becoming all You made me to be in Christ.

Having these promises, beloved, let us cleanse ourselves from all filthiness of the flesh and spirit, perfecting holiness in the fear of God.

2 CORINTHIANS 7:1

When I Need to Remember Who I Am in Christ

hank You, Jesus, that because I believe in You and have received You into my heart, I am a child of God and everything I have comes from God. You are my heavenly Father, and because of that I can move into the inheritance You have especially saved for me. Help me to understand all that You have for me so that I will be able to receive it. If there are things You have willed for my life that I am not moving in to claim, help me to understand what they are. Help me to walk in the liberty You have freed me to enjoy.

As many as received Him, to them He gave the right to become children of God, to those who believe in His name.

JOHN 1:12

When I Need to Remember Who I Am in Christ

*L*ord, I thank You that You have made me to be a partaker of Your divine nature. Thank You that because I am in Christ, I can escape the lust and corruption of the world and be preserved for Your kingdom. Thank You for Your exceedingly great and precious promises to me. Help me to hide them in my heart and remember them every day. Help me to cling to You and Your promises for my life and not to old fears or doubts. Help me to understand fully who You made me to be in Christ.

His divine power has given to us all things that pertain to life and godliness, through the knowledge of Him who called us by glory and virtue, by which have been given to us exceedingly great and precious promises, that through these you may be partakers of the divine nature, having escaped the corruption that is in the world through lust.

2 PETER 1:3-4

When I Need to Remember Who I Am in Christ

Thank You, Lord, that You won the battle over death and hell, and because of that I will always prevail over the enemy. You have lifted me above any enemy threat. Because I am in Christ, I am victorious. I am a winner. Help me to live like the victorious person You have made me to be. Help me to walk in the victory You have for me in every part of my life. Enable me to win at life so that I can fulfill the purpose for which I was created.

The LORD shall go forth like a mighty man; He shall stir up His zeal like a man of war. He shall cry out, yes, shout aloud; He shall prevail against His enemies.

ISAIAH 42:13

When I Need to Remember Who I Am in Christ

*L*ord, help me to remember that no matter what happens in my life, I belong to You. In life and in death, I am Yours. Even when I fail, stray, or do stupid things, You still love me and I am still Yours. Even when I forget to pray or read Your Word, I am still Yours. I release my life into Your hands, and wherever I have held on to my life in order to try and make things happen, I let go of all that. I want You to be in charge from now on.

If we live, we live to the Lord; and if we die, we die to the Lord. Therefore, whether we live or die, we are the Lord's.

ROMANS 14:8

When I Need to Remember Who I Am in Christ

*F*ather, help me to be more like Jesus. Help me to seek You early in the morning, just as Jesus did. Let my first thoughts be of You whenever I wake up. You have made me to be a praying person—Your child who seeks Your presence often. I know that I will never be able to understand who I am in Christ if I don't spend time alone with You the way Jesus did. Enable me to spend quality time with You throughout each day.

In the morning, having risen a long while before daylight, He went out and departed to a solitary place; and there He prayed.

MARK 1:35

When I Need to Remember Who I Am in Christ

*L*ord, I thank You that You have made me to be like the fragrance of Christ to others. Help me to bring the refreshing of Your Spirit to those who are perishing in their lack of knowledge of You and lack of understanding about Your ways. Thank You that You are a God who can be known, and You share who You are with me because I love, serve, and worship You. Help me to share all of You that You have put in me with others as well.

We are to God the fragrance of Christ among those who are being saved and among those who are perishing. To the one we are the aroma of death leading to death, and to the other the aroma of life leading to life. And who is sufficient for these things?

2 Corinthians 2:15-16

When I Need to Remember Who I Am in Christ

*L*ord, Your creation itself tells me that You are real and You are great. Your eternal power and divine nature are clear to me when I look at the things You have made. Your existence becomes undeniable when I see what You have done in my life. I acknowledge You as my Creator who not only created me, but who is continuing to create in me a heart that will do Your will. Help me to always remember that because I am a child of the God of the universe, I have a destiny that is good.

The heavens declare the glory of God; and the firmament shows His handiwork.

PSALM 19:1

When I Need to Remember Who I Am in Christ

*D*ear God, I thank You that I am renewed according to the image of Christ stamped upon my heart and mind. Help me to get rid of anything old in my life that would keep me from becoming more like You every day. Help me to put off the old person I used to be—even as recently as yesterday—and put on the new person You have made me to be in Christ. Continue to renew my mind and soul so I can be made more and more like You.

Do not lie to one another, since you have put off the old man with his deeds, and have put on the new man who is renewed in knowledge according to the image of Him who created him.

Colossians 3:8-10

When I Need to Remember Who I Am in Christ

*T*hank You, Jesus, for all You suffered on the cross to take away the consequences of my sin and rebellion and give me peace with God. Along with that I receive the total healing and restoration You paid a price for me to have. Heal my body, mind, and soul—my whole person and my whole life. Because I have been saved, I have also been spared the devastation I would have inherited without You. But with You I can be totally renewed and restored in every way.

He was wounded for our transgressions, He was bruised for our iniquities; the chastisement for our peace was upon Him, and by His stripes we are healed.

ISAIAH 53:5

When I Need Help in My Relationships

Lord, help me to achieve that great goal of always esteeming others above myself. Help me to not be selfish or prideful in my relationships in any way. Show me how to value each relationship and teach me how to demonstrate godly love for every person with whom I come in contact. Help me to be more closely yoked with people who love You and walk with You in Your ways. Help me to not think of what I can get out of a relationship, but what I can give to it.

Let nothing be done through selfish ambition or conceit, but in lowliness of mind let each esteem others better than himself.

PHILIPPIANS 2:3

When I Need Help in My Relationships

*L*ord, when one of the greatest disappointments in my life is a person, I pray You would help me to release him or her, and the memory of what they did or did not do, to You. I don't want to carry around grief and sadness like a burden, because it is too heavy for me to bear. I yoke up with You instead and ask You to carry that burden for me. I release the burden of that relationship into Your hands right now. I don't want to live in the darkness of bitterness and unforgiveness. I want to live in Your light where I will not stumble.

He who says he is in the light, and hates his brother, is in darkness until now. He who loves his brother abides in the light, and there is no cause for stumbling in him.

1 JOHN 2:9-10

When I Need Help in My Relationships

*L*ord, help me to move in Your love with regard to other people in my life. Help me to come to an agreement and be like-minded with people who are godly. Help us to be in unity with one another. If we all have the mind of Christ and the same Holy Spirit living in us, this shouldn't be hard to do, unless one of us moves in the flesh and not the Spirit. Help me to always move in the Spirit with regard to my relationships and refuse to be self-centered.

Fulfill my joy by being like-minded, having the same love, being of one accord, of one mind.

PHILIPPIANS 2:2

When I Need Help in My Relationships

*D*ear God, I ask that You would help me to do whatever it takes to have peaceful relationships. Where there are problems with a person, help me to show love. Where I have been hurt by someone, help me to forgive. Keep me from ever doing anything vengeful. Help me to release any difficult relationships I have into Your hands and not try to fix them on my own. I rely on You because You are the only one who can transform a difficult relationship.

If it is possible, as much as depends on you, live peaceably with all men. Beloved, do not avenge yourselves, but rather give place to wrath; for it is written, "Vengeance is Mine, I will repay," says the Lord.

ROMANS 12:18-19

When I Need Help
in My Relationships

*D*ear Lord, help me to have great compassion for others, especially my brothers and sisters in Christ. Help me to be loving and tenderhearted, kind and courteous. Show me when I am not. Reveal to me how my words and actions affect other people so that I can always be a blessing. In my most difficult relationship I pray that Your peace would reign. Take away all strife so that we can come to a meeting of our minds as well as a joining of our hearts.

All of you be of one mind, having compassion for one another; love as brothers, be tenderhearted, be courteous.

1 PETER 3:8

When I Need Help in My Relationships

*L*ord, I pray that You would help me to be at peace with all people in my life. Deliver me from strife in any relationship. I pray for all my relationships to have a deep element of Your peace flowing through them. Help me to be holy as You are holy, so that I become someone people enjoy being around. Help me to always reflect Your love and grace to others. Show me how I can be a blessing to the people in my life today.

Pursue peace with all people, and holiness, without which no one will see the Lord.

HEBREWS 12:14

When I Need Help in My Relationships

*L*ord, help me to be a friend who loves at all times. When things happen that are troublesome and disturbing in my relationships, help me to look above the problem to You. Help me to see the positive in the conflict and the good You will bring out of it. Help me to focus on Your mighty power that can transform a relationship in a moment. Where there has been a breech in a relationship, I pray that You would not only repair it, but You would make the relationship better. If this is a relationship I am to let go of, help me to do that. I know that if this is Your will, You will bring the healing needed to move on.

A friend loves at all times, and a brother is born for adversity.

PROVERBS 17:17

When I Need Help in My Relationships

*L*ord, help me to choose my friends carefully so that I never become the companion of a foolish person. Help me to walk with godly and wise people so that I can become like them. When something happens that is disturbing to me in a friendship, I pray that You will turn it around for good and bring something positive out of it. I ask that You would do good things in all my relationships, especially bless those that seem difficult.

He who walks with wise men will be wise, but the companion of fools will be destroyed.

PROVERBS 13:20

When I Need Help in My Relationships

*L*ord, whenever grief over something that has happened to people I care about tries to come back and torture me, I ask that You would take it from me and give me Your peace. Help me to rise above those feelings and see that life goes on because You go on forever. Wherever there has been a loss of a relationship, heal me of that emptiness. Take away the sad memories and help me to remember the good things. Give me a strong vision for the future so that I can focus on that. Enable me to comfort those who grieve in the same way you have comforted me.

Blessed are those who mourn, for they shall be comforted.

MATTHEW 5:4

When I Need Help in My Relationships

$\mathcal{D}$ear Lord, I pray You would help me to be the kind of friend who is a sure help in times of trouble. I know that strong, committed friendships are important for everyone because You have said that it is not good for us to be alone. Help me to find friends who are as committed to me as I am to them. Help us to be a mutual support to one another, always pointing each other toward a deeper walk with You.

Two are better than one, because they have a good reward for their labor. For if they fall, one will lift up his companion. But woe to him who is alone when he falls, for he has no one to help him up.

ECCLESIASTES 4:9-10

When I Need Help
in My Relationships

*L*ord, help me to have good, godly friendships with other believers so that we will be people who walk by the same rules. Help me to be with those who are like-minded in our love of Your Word and our devotion to living Your way. I pray for the relationships I already have, that they would be glorifying to You. For any friend I have who doesn't know You, I pray that You would bring them to a saving knowledge of Christ. Help me to be a strong, godly influence on them.

To the degree that we have already attained, let us walk by the same rule, let us be of the same mind.

PHILIPPIANS 3:16

When I Need Help in My Relationships

*D*ear God, I pray I will not be unequally yoked with an unbeliever. Where that is already the case, I pray You would bring that person to know You as their Savior or else free me from the relationship. Where I have been influenced by unbelievers in ways that are not good, help me to identify and correct it. Help me to be such a good influence on others that I am able to draw unbelievers to You with the godliness they see in me.

Do not be unequally yoked together with unbelievers. For what fellowship has righteousness with lawlessness? And what communion has light with darkness? And what accord has Christ with Belial? Or what part has a believer with an unbeliever?

2 CORINTHIANS 6:14-15

When I Need Help in My Relationships

*D*ear Lord, I pray You would send godly friends into my life who will be a good influence on me, who will sharpen my mind and soul, and strengthen my walk with You. May they be friends who will challenge me to grow in the things of Your kingdom and who will stand by me when I go through difficult times. Help me to be that same kind of friend—one who stands by others in their time of need. I know that having godly friends is extremely important when it comes to finding fulfillment and wholeness in my life.

As iron sharpens iron, so a man sharpens the countenance of his friend.

PROVERBS 27:17

When I Need Help in My Relationships

*D*ear God, I pray that You would make me to be a peacemaker among people. Show me how to always speak the right words to bring peace to a situation or a relationship. Help me to also be a peace*keeper*. Give me the ability to maintain peace in a relationship once peace has been established. Teach me the ways of peace so I can always see what needs to happen in order to establish it. You have called me to peace. Help me to fulfill that calling in every way possible. I pray for Your peace to reign in all my relationships.

God has called us to peace.

1 Corinthians 7:15

When I Need to Feel Close to God

*D*ear Lord, I long for Your presence more than anything else on earth. My number one priority in life is You. My relationship with You is the fountainhead from which my life flows. Without You I have nothing, because without You all else is meaningless and futile. Help me to always seek You first before all else. I hunger after you and ask that You would fill any emptiness in my heart today with more of You. I seek Your refreshing in the dry areas of my soul. Pour into me Your living water—a fresh filling of Your Holy Spirit this day.

O God, You are my God; early will I seek You; my soul thirsts for You; my flesh longs for You in a dry and thirsty land where there is no water.

PSALM 63:1

When I Need to Feel Close to God

*L*ord, thank You that You are close to all who call on You. I call on You right now and ask for a special sense of Your presence. I want to be closer to You than ever and feel Your presence cast away all oppression, doubt, or instability. Thank You that You are a God who can be found, who draws near to those who draw near to Him. I draw near to You today because I can't live without You in my life.

Seek the LORD while He may be found, call upon Him while He is near.

ISAIAH 55:6

When I Need to
Feel Close to God

*L*ord, I shut out all else from my life right now and draw close to You. I release my worries and concerns into Your hands. I let them go and lay them at Your feet. I share with You the secrets of my heart and ask You to share with me the secrets of Yours. Fill me afresh with Your Spirit so that I can enjoy Your love, peace, joy, and fulfillment in my life in greater measure than ever before.

When you pray, go into your room, and when you have shut your door, pray to your Father who is in the secret place; and your Father who sees in secret will reward you openly.

MATTHEW 6:6

When I Need to Feel Close to God

*L*ord, I don't want anything to come between You and me. I especially don't want my own carelessness in the way I live to cause a separation between us. Help me to obey You and live Your way so that You will always hear my prayers. Show me any hidden sin in my life, and I will confess and repent of whatever You reveal to me. I want to get rid of anything that keeps me from a close walk with You.

Your iniquities have separated you from your God; and your sins have hidden His face from you, so that He will not hear.

ISAIAH 59:2

When I Need to Feel Close to God

Lord, just as David worshipped You often, I know that I can't get very far in life without stopping to worship You too. Right now I worship You for all that You are, and I praise You for all You have done for me. I thank You with my whole heart for Your presence in my life, and I will continue to praise You every day, as often as I think of You. Enable me to worship and praise You in a way that is pleasing in Your sight.

David went and brought up the ark of God from the house of Obed-Edom to the City of David with gladness. And so it was, when those bearing the ark of the LORD had gone six paces, that he sacrificed oxen and fatted sheep.

2 SAMUEL 6:12-13

When I Need to Feel Close to God

*L*ord, I welcome Your presence right now in my heart and my mind. I invite You to be enthroned in every area of my life today and every day that I am on this earth. I know that in Your presence I will find healing and wholeness. Outside of Your presence I have no life. Outside of Your presence I cannot accomplish anything of any lasting value. Help me to never be separated from Your presence by any foolish thoughts or disobedience to Your ways. Help me to praise you often and walk close to You at all times.

Although they knew God, they did not glorify Him as God, nor were thankful, but became futile in their thoughts, and their foolish hearts were darkened.

ROMANS 1:21

When I Need to Feel Close to God

*L*ord, I praise You in the morning when I get up, in the evening before I go to sleep, and all times in between. Help me to make praise to You the first thing that comes out of my mouth whenever I wake up—even in the middle of the night. Help me to overflow with praise for who You are and all You have done. And when I come to the time when I have only one prayer left, may it be a prayer of praise and worship to You.

From the rising of the sun to its going down the LORD'*s name is to be praised.*

PSALM 113:3

When I Need to Feel Close to God

*L*ord, instead of focusing on myself and my problems, I want to focus on You and Your greatness. Instead of dwelling on my needs, I want to dwell on Your supply and give thanks to You for all You have already given me. I praise You and thank You for Your grace, mercy, love, peace, joy, power, and rest. I draw close to You and invite Your presence with my praise. In Your presence I have everything I will ever need.

Oh, give thanks to the LORD, for He is good! For His mercy endures forever.

PSALM 118:1

When I Need to
Feel Close to God

*D*ear Lord, I thank You that You have made Yourself available to me. By simply drawing close to You, You will draw close to me. I come close to You now and ask that You would give me a deep sense of Your presence. Sometimes I feel that my life is too much for me to handle, and there are too many expectations I can't live up to, and there are too many frightening possibilities. At those times I need to be close to You more than ever. I need to hear Your voice speaking to my heart that everything will be okay. Help me to see my life from Your perspective.

Draw near to God and He will draw near to you.

JAMES 4:8

When I Need to Feel Close to God

*L*ord, I worship You and exalt You above all else in my life. Reveal Yourself to me in new and wonderful ways, because I need to know You better. You are all-powerful and all-wonderful, and it gives me joy to worship You. Thank You, Lord, that as I draw close to You, You teach my mind, soul, and spirit things I need to know. Help me to live in Your presence where healing and wholeness happen. I know that things work out when I spend time with You.

Who is the man that fears the LORD? Him shall He teach in the way He chooses. He himself shall dwell in prosperity, and his descendants shall inherit the earth. The secret of the LORD is with those who fear Him, and He will show them His covenant.

PSALM 25:12-14

When I Need to Feel Close to God

*L*ord, I seek Your face this day because I long to be with You like a friend. I long to walk with You and spend time talking to You. I need to hear You and know that You hear me. Help me to live in Your presence more and more, for it is only there that I can find the peace that passes all understanding. I praise Your holy name, for You are my Savior, healer, deliverer, and provider. You are the Almighty God of the universe who restores my soul to wholeness.

Glory in His holy name; let the hearts of those rejoice who seek the Lord! Seek the Lord and His strength; seek His face evermore! Remember His marvelous works which He has done, His wonders, and the judgments of His mouth.

1 Chronicles 16:10-12

When I Need to Feel Close to God

*D*ear Lord, I thank You that I can never be separated from You. No matter where I go, You are there. Even if I am lost to all other people on earth, You still know where I am. There is no place where You cannot find me or see me. Help me to remember this whenever I feel lost or distant from You. Help me to know that You are always as close to me as I invite You to be.

Trust in Him at all times, you people; pour out your heart before Him; God is a refuge for us.

PSALM 62:8

When I Need to Feel Close to God

*H*eavenly Father, in the night when I feel anxious about things and I'm tired and overwhelmed with all that I face, it's then I long for Your presence more than ever. My soul and spirit seek Your Holy Spirit—my Comforter and Helper—to ease my mind. I am so grateful that every time I seek You, You can be found. Help me to remember to always run to You at the first sign of emptiness so I can be comforted, strengthened, calmed, and filled afresh with Your Holy Spirit.

With my soul I have desired You in the night, yes, by my spirit within me I will seek You early; for when Your judgments are in the earth, the inhabitants of the world will learn righteousness.

ISAIAH 26:9

When I Need to Feel Close to God

*T*hank You, Lord, for who You are in my life. I reverence You above all else in this world. I know that in my worship, praise, and awe of You there is a flow of Your Spirit that is released to me that brings life. It allows Your life to flow into mine. This flow of life carries me away from the pitfalls of destruction and death. Praising You takes me closer to You, where I can find that fountain of life that is the flow of Your Spirit. Wash over me and through me right now, Lord, and give me new life.

The fear of the LORD is a fountain of life, to turn one away from the snares of death.

PROVERBS 14:27

When I Need to Understand My Purpose and My Future

*L*ord, help me to have patience and not grow weary or discouraged while waiting for answers to my prayers and for things to happen. Whenever I have doubt about my future, help me to remember that I have a high purpose and calling. When I can't see how the future is ever going to turn out the way I want it to, help me to remember that because I have given my life to You, my future will turn out like *You* want it to. You have promised me a future of peace and hope, a future far greater than I can imagine. Thank You, Lord, for thinking of me.

"I know the thoughts that I think toward you," says the LORD, *"thoughts of peace and not of evil, to give you a future and a hope."*

JEREMIAH 29:11

When I Need to Understand My Purpose and My Future

*L*ord, help me to be a person who brings the good news of Your salvation to others. Enable me to bring Your peace and deliverance to those who need it. Give me the ability to forget about my own needs and concentrate on helping to meet the needs of others. Show me how to proclaim Your kingdom wherever I go. Just as You reign on earth, I ask You to also reign in my heart. Rule in my life and take me into the future You have for me.

How beautiful upon the mountains are the feet of him who brings good news, who proclaims peace, who brings glad tidings of good things, who proclaims salvation, who says to Zion, "Your God reigns!"

Isaiah 52:7

When I Need to Understand My Purpose and My Future

*L*ord, I know that You have created me with a unique gifting and a specific calling. Help me to understand what that is. You have given me a special purpose. Help me to move into it. You have established for me a future that is good. Help me to trust You about that, especially when the future seems unsure or frightening. Help me to always lift up praise to You and thank You for all that You have ahead for me. Thank You that I will never lose the calling and purpose You have for my life. Thank You for freedom to be who You created me to be.

He who is called in the Lord while a slave is the Lord's freedman. Likewise he who is called while free is Christ's slave.

1 CORINTHIANS 7:22

When I Need to Understand My Purpose and My Future

*L*ord, I thank You that Your promises never fail. I see that illustrated in Your Word in each of Your servants through whom Your amazing promises were fulfilled. I pray that You would fulfill Your promises in me. Thank You that You have promised me provision and protection and the fulfillment of my purpose. Thank You that You have promised me eternal life with You. I trust You for *all* of Your promises, and I thank You that even now they are being fulfilled in my life.

Blessed be the Lord, who has given rest to His people Israel, according to all that He promised. There has not failed one word of all His good promise, which He promised through His servant Moses.

1 Kings 8:56

When I Need to Understand My Purpose and My Future

*L*ord, help me to believe for the great future You have promised to me. Help me to prepare for it by taking steps of faith that You show me. Help me to grow in all areas of my life and to expand my expectations of You so that there is room for You to fill my life with all that You have for me. I pray that my life will be built on a solid rock that can never be moved. And even into old age I pray that I will still have to expand my horizons to hold the blessings You will pour into my life.

Enlarge the place of your tent, and let them stretch out the curtains of your dwellings; do not spare; lengthen your cords, and strengthen your stakes. For you shall expand to the right and to the left, and your descendants will inherit the nations, and make the desolate cities inhabited.

ISAIAH 54:2-3

When I Need to Understand My Purpose and My Future

Lord, I know that my purpose is to be Your love manifested toward others. Help me to do that. Show me how. Prepare my heart to be Your hand extended. Help me to lead others to You and show them how Your ways make life work. Enable me to help those who are suffering and without hope. Help me to give to those in need. Make me bold to speak the truth of Your salvation and hope as Your Spirit leads me.

Let each of you look out not only for his own interests, but also for the interests of others.

PHILIPPIANS 2:4

When I Need to Understand My Purpose and My Future

*L*ord, I thank You that because I believe in You, my future is secure. Not only my future here on earth, but my eternal future with You in heaven. Whether I live or die, my future is secure. Help me to remember that at all times so that I will not fear death when it comes. Thank You, Lord, that You are the bread of life and You sustain me in every way. I don't have to worry about the future, because You know my needs and are ready to meet them even before I ask.

Most assuredly, I say to you, he who believes in Me has everlasting life. I am the bread of life.

JOHN 6:47-48

When I Need to Understand My Purpose and My Future

*T*hank You, Lord, for Your abounding grace in my life. Because of Your grace, I have everything I need in order to make life work. I want to do significant and meaningful things to bless others and make positive changes that last. Help me to accomplish great things for Your glory. I ask that You would provide me with everything I need in life so that I will have an abundance for every good work that You want me to do.

God is able to make all grace abound toward you, that you, always having all sufficiency in all things, may have an abundance for every good work.

2 CORINTHIANS 9:8

When I Need to Understand My Purpose and My Future

$\mathcal{L}$ord, make me ready to do Your will and move into the purpose for which I was created. Send me out with joy to do Your work. Lead me with peace. Help me to follow You in all things so I can accomplish Your perfect will. Help me to hear the celebration of Your creation as I lift up praise and worship to You over the great things You will do in me, through me, and around me.

You shall go out with joy, and be led out with peace; the mountains and the hills shall break forth into singing before you, and all the trees of the field shall clap their hands.

ISAIAH 55:12

When I Need to Understand My Purpose and My Future

*D*ear God, help me to have the strength I need to endure all the challenges I must face in my future. I want to do Your will and fulfill the purpose for which I was created. I want to move into the future You have for me. I want to receive all of the promises You have for my life. But I know that doesn't just happen. I must be diligent to pray and determined to obey You at all times. Help me to do that. Thank You, Lord, that after I have done Your will, I shall receive Your promises for my future, both here and in eternity.

For you have need of endurance, so that after you have done the will of God, you may receive the promise.

HEBREWS 10:36

When I Need to Understand My Purpose and My Future

*L*ord, I thank You for Your promise of eternity in heaven for all who love You and proclaim You as Lord over their life. Help me to keep eternity in my perspective as I move forward on the path You have for me and into the future for which I was created. Help me to serve You faithfully all my days, until such time as I come to spend forever with You. Eternal life in Your kingdom is the greatest promise of all, and I praise You for the sacrifice it took for You to secure that for me.

This is the promise that He has promised us— eternal life.

1 JOHN 2:25

When I Need to Understand My Purpose and My Future

*L*ord, speak to me of my future. Holy Spirit of truth, teach me the truth about my life and my purpose. Tell me something about what is ahead so that I can have rest in my soul about it. Give me a vision for my future that assures me it is secure. Help me to have joyful anticipation about it. Even though You may not reveal the details of it, help me to see that I have a good future to look forward to.

When He, the Spirit of truth, has come, He will guide you into all truth; for He will not speak on His own authority, but whatever He hears He will speak; and He will tell you things to come.

JOHN 16:13

When I Need to Understand My Purpose and My Future

*D*ear Lord, I am so grateful that You will do more in my life than I can even imagine. Your Word says that what You have for me is "exceedingly abundantly" above all that I can ask or think. This is amazing to me, Lord, because I can think of and ask for a great deal. With great anticipation I look forward to all You have ahead for me in my future. Help me to not get in the way of anything You want to do in me and through me.

To Him who is able to do exceedingly abundantly above all that we ask or think, according to the power that works in us, to Him be glory in the church by Christ Jesus to all generations, forever and ever. Amen.

EPHESIANS 3:20-21

When I Need to Understand My Purpose and My Future

Lord, help me to not be discouraged when it seems as though I don't see fruit in my life. I know You are the source of all fruitfulness. I praise You and invite You to release Your life-begetting power in me. I pray You will make every barren area in my life to be fruitful and productive. When I start to feel that I may never give birth to anything of significance, I will lift up praise to You, because it is only through Your enablement that I can break forth into the purpose for which You have called me.

"Sing, O barren, you who have not borne! Break forth into singing, and cry aloud, you who have not labored with child! For more are the children of the desolate than the children of the married woman," says the LORD.

ISAIAH 54:1

When I Need to Understand My Purpose and My Future

Dear God, unless You teach me, I will not know the right way to go. Unless You speak to me from Your Word, I cannot fully understand Your ways. Holy Spirit, guide me in all things and give me wisdom. Purify my heart and make me more like You each day so that I can become all You created me to be. I wait on You to lead me on into the future You have for me. I don't want to take one step without You.

Show me Your ways, O Lord; teach me Your paths.
Lead me in Your truth and teach me, for You are the
God of my salvation; on You I wait all the day.

PSALM 25:4-5

When I Need to Understand My Purpose and My Future

$\mathscr{L}$ord, help me to forget all that is behind me so that I can reach forward to the future You have for me. My main goal in life is to fulfill Your calling. Help me to do that. Help me to run the race well, to fight the good fight, to not compromise the life You have for me in any way. Help me to not look back into the past where I let fear, doubt, and ignorance of Your ways influence the decisions I made. Enable me to rise above all that into the complete wholeness and purpose You have for my life.

I do not count myself to have apprehended; but one thing I do, forgetting those things which are behind and reaching forward to those things which are ahead, I press toward the goal for the prize of the upward call of God in Christ Jesus.

PHILIPPIANS 3:13-14

Prayer Journal

> *"Lord, teach me how to pray for my adult children. I know You are greater than anything they face. Thank You that my prayers for them have power because You hear me and will answer. I pray You will guide and protect them and help them to become all they were created to be."*

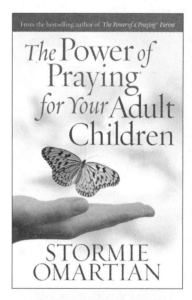

Perhaps you are watching your grown children step out into the world and wishing you could do more to support them while giving them the freedom they crave. You can. It doesn't matter how young or old they are, you can rest in the power of God working through your prayers.

In this important follow-up to *The Power of a Praying® Parent* (more than 1.7 million sold), Stormie Omartian addresses your unique concerns as a parent of grown children. She also shares how you can confidently lift them up to God. With stories from other parents and insight gleaned from personal experience, Stormie provides fresh insight on praying with the power of God's Word over your adult children and their

- career choices and sense of purpose
- marriages and other vital relationships
- parenting skills and leadership roles
- financial struggles and emotional trials
- faith, health, and ability to make good decisions

From the bestselling author of The Power of a Praying® Parent

The Power of Praying for Your Adult Children

STORMIE OMARTIAN

"When we take our concerns to the Lord—trusting that God hears our prayers and answers them on behalf of our adult children—it means our prayers have power to effect change in their lives," says Stormie. "And that gives us a peace we can find no other way."

The Power of a Praying® Woman

Bestselling author Stormie Omartian's deep knowledge of Scripture and candid examples from her own prayer life provide guidance for women who seek to trust God with deep longings, cover every area of life with prayer, and maintain a right heart before God. Each segment concludes with a prayer women can follow or use as a model for their own prayers. Women will find hope and purpose as they give their lives over to God.

Just Enough Light for the Step I'm On

People facing life changes, difficult times, or the pressures of today's world will appreciate Stormie's honesty and candor based on experience and the Word of God in this book of comfort, encouragement, and sound advice. It's about learning how to trust God to provide all that you need in every situation.

The Power of Prayer to Change Your Marriage

Stormie Omartian's bestselling books on prayer and marriage have touched millions of readers in a life-changing way. *The Power of Prayer to Change Your Marriage* helps husbands or wives pray to protect their relationship from 14 serious problems that can lead to unsatisfying marriages or even divorce. For those who are already struggling in these areas, this book will help them find healing and restoration.

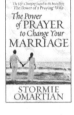

www.stormieomartian.com

To learn more about Harvest House books and
to read sample chapters, log on to our website:

www.harvesthousepublishers.com

HARVEST HOUSE PUBLISHERS
EUGENE, OREGON